Misfit Faith

Misfit Faith

Confessions of a Drunk Ex-Pastor

JASON J. STELLMAN

Convergent

New York

Published in the United States by Convergent Books, an imprint of
the Crown Publishing Group, a division of Penguin Random House
LLC, New York.
crownpublishing.com

CONVERGENT BOOKS is a registered trademark and the
C colophon is a trademark of Penguin Random House LLC.

Library of Congress Cataloging-in-Publication Data is available upon
request.

ISBN 978-0-8041-4062-1
Ebook ISBN 978-0-8041-4061-4

Printed in the United States of America

Jacket design by Keenan

10 9 8 7 6 5 4 3 2 1

First Edition

This book is dedicated to the listeners of

Drunk Ex-Pastors—hitting the "record" button and

allowing you all into our discussions and lives has been one of the

most rewarding things I've ever done.

And to Christian Kingery, my cohost, best friend, and

the most genuine guy I know. I don't think there is

a single statement in this book that we didn't argue

about at some point, both on and off the air.

Thank you. But the royalties are all mine.

Contents

//

Introduction

(Or, I Once Was Found, But Now I'm Lost)

I used to be a pastor, but I'm not anymore. I used to have the respect of a congregation and colleagues in ministry, but I don't anymore. I used to be able to pay my bills, but I can't anymore. (In fact, the very day I had my first phone conversation with my publisher's marketing department about this book was the day I was approved for food stamps. Those benefits were since slashed to almost nothing.) I'm *this* close to saying that "I used to believe in God, but I don't anymore," but I can't. Call me stubborn, but I do still believe in him, despite an alarming amount of evidence that he doesn't believe in me. I suppose what this makes me is a misfit. And if you're reading this book, chances are you're one too. So I hope you're okay with hearing confessions, because there's some stuff I need to get off my chest.

As usual, G. K. Chesterton said it best: "If a thing is

worth doing, it is worth doing badly." I heartily agree and have taken up this maxim and made it into something of a motto for my own life (although my version of it is more along the lines of "I'd rather suck at something awesome than be awesome at something that sucks"). So true to form, I am now a really bad Catholic. But in a spirit of perverse paradox, I can't help but wonder if perhaps Christianity is done best when done poorly. I mean, a lot of water has flowed under a lot of bridges since Jesus was around, and admiring him has gotten pretty complex and difficult over the last couple of millennia. Don't get me wrong, I appreciate details and dogma as much as the next guy, but as someone who has little patience these days for spiritual correctness (having learned my lesson), I have just found that stripping things back to basics results in a faith that, despite not really fitting any prior mold, is simple enough to actually practice. I suppose that's what this book is all about: When misfits try to have faith, it's only a matter of time until they screw it all up. But unlike spinal surgery or online banking, there's a certain beauty in imprecision and inexactitude when applied to Christianity. Doing it wrong is sort of an indirect way of doing it right, while those who actually think they're doing it right are mostly just complete tools that not even Jesus can stand. "Misfit Faith," then, is kind of shorthand for the Christianity practiced by those who've learned the hard way that there is no easy way, who have no other hope than the last being first, and who have discovered that failing at the best thing is itself an ironic success.

But before we get into all that, some background.

My Days as a Crap Baptist

I grew up in a relatively nonreligious home. My parents were pretty good at insisting that we drag ourselves to church every Christmas Eve and Easter whether we needed it or not, but apart from that there wasn't much happening piety-wise. (Not that there was a lot of impiety, either.) Suffice it to say that I had a pretty typical experience as a child growing up in southern California in the 1980s: I went to school, played sports, watched *Star Wars,* and surfed and skateboarded.

Things changed a bit when I was in the sixth grade, however. Some neighbors of ours were members of a local Baptist church with an Awana program. (For those unfamiliar, Awana is like Scouts with way less camping and way more Bible.) For some reason still unknown to me, my parents decided that it was about time my brother and I "got some religion," so off we went to join Awana and, eventually, Fountain Valley Baptist Church.

During one of our Wednesday night meetings, my fellow sixth-graders and I were subjected to a story about a little boy who came home from school and found his house empty and all his family missing. (I think his dog was gone too, but

I can't confirm this.) Those of you with Baptist upbringings can surely guess what little Billy came to discover, albeit too late: the Rapture had taken place, and Billy had been left behind! Needless to say, the story of a boy my age entering the Great Tribulation as a petless orphan had the desired effect on me, and once the meeting was over, I grabbed my friend Gary, whose father was a leader in the church, and asked him how to become a Christian. "Dude, it's so easy," he assured me. "I mean, I became one *in the car* on the way to church when I was little!" Since Gary was about the best Christian kid I knew, I placed my destiny in his hands and asked him to help me become a believer so that I wouldn't miss the Rapture like Billy in the story. He told me to close my eyes and repeat a prayer after him. Upon uttering the final "amen," I looked at him and said, "You're full of it! I'm finding a grown-up who can help me do this right," and off I went to solicit the aid of an actual adult (who, as it turned out, led me in the exact same prayer that Gary did. I guess Gary was either quite sophisticated, or the grown-up quite unsophisticated, for his age, I'm not sure which). Upon successfully asking Jesus to come live in my heart (for the second time), I was given a Bible, enrolled somewhat against my will in what I now understand was a new believers class (although at the time I had no idea why they kept pulling me out of my normal Sunday school class and sticking me in a class with a bunch of people I didn't know), and baptized by immersion after giving my testimony in front of the congregation. From that point on, whether my life reflected it or not (it didn't), I considered and called myself a Christian.

The next few years showed little growth in my Christian walk, if any. Awana ends after sixth grade, but like the rest of my friends, I joined the junior high group at church, and the high school group after that. If memory serves, these meetings were pretty gimmicky and shallow—there'd be some kind of game or exercise we'd do, and then *bam!*, a spiritual lesson to tie it all together. (Who knew *that* was coming?) But to their credit, at least there were no trust-falls.

During this early teenage period, I developed a rather cutting and acerbic sense of humor, which was honed mainly by watching and rewatching *Fletch* (I also read all the books on which the film was based), as well as the standard John Hughes movies that defined the 1980s so poignantly. My friends and I would egg each other on to see who could be the most sarcastic and down-putting of others, which eventually led to a split in the youth group, with us "cool kids" forming our own little gathering under the guidance of one of the youth leaders. He also liked *Fletch,* so it was fine.

Plenty of other hijinks ensued, some more serious than others. The youth group kids would sit together during church rather than with our parents, which afforded us the freedom to screw around during communion, clinking our thimble-size cups together and saying "Down the hatch!" before drinking the wine (excuse me, grape juice). Or, we'd duck out for a bathroom break during the sermon and sneak across the street to 7-Eleven, where we would buy Big Gulps. (Actually that's not entirely true. What we would do is put a small cup inside a Big Gulp cup and fill the small one with soda while filling the area around it with candy. Once you put the lid on, it looked like a large drink instead of a smuggling device for Snickers and Skittles.)

The highlights of my spiritual life usually occurred during our high school group's annual trip to Hume Lake, a youth-oriented Christian camp in the mountains of California. The week-long excursion consisted of mostly hype—games, challenges, Christian rock music, and so on. To quote Maverick from the 1986 film *Top Gun,* Hume Lake was truly a "target-rich environment," and therefore the week would inevitably begin for my friends and me with the goal of meeting good-looking girls from other churches' youth groups. Once the girlfriend-for-the-week was secured, we would then proceed to more spiritually profitable activities, like vowing to destroy all our secular music (a promise that took about a week to break). But as at most youth camps, by the end of the week prayers were prayed, vows were made, sins were written on slips of paper and thrown into the campfire, and we all promised ourselves that we'd continue to be good boys and girls once we got back "down the mountain." (But we didn't.)

Things continued on in pretty much the same way until my junior year of high school, when I informed my parents that I wanted to transfer from my current public school, Dana Hills (or Dana *Pills,* as it was sometimes called because of its hearty-partying student body), and begin attending Calvary

Chapel High School in Costa Mesa, where a couple of friends from our Baptist church had recently transferred. This took a little convincing, but my parents eventually acquiesced, and thus began my relationship with megachurch evangelicalism. (Though Calvary Chapel of Costa Mesa has no membership and thus cannot keep track of its attendance with any precision, conservative estimates say that upward of ten thousand people walk through its doors in a given week.)

I brought my glib and cavalier attitude toward Christianity with me to Calvary Chapel. It didn't take long to discover that Calvary kids took their faith pretty seriously. I still remember how weird it sounded hearing other teenagers use phrases like "the Lord laid it on my heart" or "I just want to get in the Word." My initial reaction was to quietly mock these people, so I did (and sometimes not so quietly). But after a heart-to-heart with the youth pastor and the "peer pressure" to be holy, well, it all just kind of clicked for me. I began to attend as many Bible studies as I could, I began to study Scripture on my own, I began to pray, and I began to seek out the fellowship of other believers. Church for me became the place where my faith was nourished and strengthened.

Dabbling in Antiquity

Yet even during this period I was a pretty old-school type of guy. I was drawn to what can be dubbed "golden ages" of times past, more historic and deeply rooted expressions of the faith. The problem was, I had very little actual frame of reference for such historical inquiry. As a new believer with modern evangelical glasses on, and as a part of a spiritual movement that began around the time Beatlemania hit, I had no real ability to think back much further than that. This resulted in my longing for the good ol' days being ful-filled by discovering the music of the Jesus People revivals of the 1960s. So there I was, a sixteen-year-old in the early 1990s, saying things like "The Christianity of today is so watered down! If you want to discover the true beauty of the faith you've gotta dig deep into the rich traditions of the past, like, all the way back to 1968." So as I cruised around Orange County in my '65 VW bus with long hair listening to bands like Love Song and Mustard Seed Faith, I truly thought I had unearthed a long-forgotten storehouse of truth and treasure. *Suck it, Stryper.*

I distinctly remember one of my first real forays into ancient (read: pre-1960s) Christianity. I was on an all-day layover in Brussels with two friends on our way to Uganda as missionaries with Calvary Chapel, and after eating some Belgian waffles (or as they're called over there, "waffles"), we happened upon St. Michael's Cathedral. We decided to check it out, and to this day its effect on me is still felt. For starters, inside some classical orchestra was going through a rehearsal at the time, which added to the beauty of what I was beholding. And as for the cathedral itself, well, it was much like any of the old cathedrals of Europe: stonework, ornate stained glass, a high altar, and the feel of majesty and memory. But for me at the age of eighteen, it was the first time I had experienced such a place—all the churches I had known in southern California looked like glorified houses, converted supermarkets, or corporate office buildings. Like modern-day Puritans, we prided ourselves on shedding the religious pomp and trappings of the past (and were rather self-congratulatory about it, I might add), but what such iconoclasm left us with was quite hollow and superficial. So touring this magnificent old place of worship awakened in me a longing for an ecclesial substance and depth that the happy-clappy evangelicalism of southern California couldn't provide.

A similar desire arose when, as a missionary a few years later in Budapest, I began to read books by Catholic philosopher Peter Kreeft. There was just something about the way he—as well as others I was reading at the time, like C. S. Lewis and J. R. R. Tolkien—spoke about the Christian faith that touched a nerve deep within me. Although I couldn't pinpoint exactly what it was, I knew that those men had something I didn't, and I wanted to figure out what it was. In fact, I wrote the following in my journal on February 21, 1996:

> To me, so often my relationship with God is so theoretical and abstract. To Catholics (or people with a Catholic influence), God is very real. He is more than a formula or a systematic theology, he has reality, substance, texture. He is not "that which we have learned about in Bible study, which our minds have

grasped," he is "that which we have seen with our eyes and heard with our ears and felt with our hearts, and that which our hands have handled." I want that very much.

About six months later I accepted John Calvin into my heart and eventually became a full-blown Presbyterian minister, and while my brief love affair with Catholicism ceased for the time being, my appreciation for things ancient only grew.

First Cracks in the Calvinist Foundation

My newfound Calvinism resulted in my getting rather unceremoniously kicked out of Calvary Chapel (where *Calvinism* was a kind of theological F-word). Upon moving back to southern California, I finished my requisite undergrad work in order to enroll at Westminster Seminary in San Diego. There I received rigorous training in theology and church history, as well as in Hebrew and Greek so I could exegete Scripture in its original languages. For the first time in my Christian life, I felt like I had it all pretty much figured out: I had a good grasp of issues like the atoning work of Christ, the function of baptism and the Lord's Supper, and the purpose and role of the church. I knew how to read the individual parts of the Bible in the light of the whole redemptive story, as well as preach Christ faithfully from any portion of Scripture. In a word, I was about as comfortable in my Protestant shoes as anyone could hope to be. And moreover, the church I planted and began to pastor in 2006, Exile Presbyterian, experienced immediate growth and actually became financially self-sustaining about six months after we opened our doors. We had a great team of leaders and elders, strong attendance, and enough money to pay my salary, our rent, and all our other expenses too (quite easily). I even had a popular theological blog with between five hundred and a thousand individual daily readers, and I was writing books and articles for popular and well-respected Protestant publishing houses.

The reason I go out of my way to bring all this up is that whenever a Calvinist Protestant "popes" (or joins the synagogue of Satan, or gives in to the dark side of the Force, or whatever other phrase denoting becoming Catholic you prefer)—especially if he is something of a public figure—a series of self-appointed psychologists begin to offer their varying diagnoses. "Oh, the reason he switched teams is that things weren't going that well for him in the Protestant world"; "He jumped ship because he was getting bored and needed a change of scenery"; "He couldn't hack it as a pastor, and that's why he bailed," and so on. You get the idea. But despite the fact that no one believed me at the time (and many still don't), the truth is that I was perfectly content in my Protestant life and ministry: I wasn't struggling with my beliefs, I wasn't hurting for money, I wasn't "dying on the vine" as the saying goes. As I said, I was perfectly content to preach, write, and pastor for the rest of my life.

But that's when things started to spin out of control, and yet this process has been anything but a simple journey from one destination to another, from Geneva to Rome, as it were. My exposure to new ideas, the wrestling that has occurred in my own soul (both with God and with myself), my crap morality, as well as the personal upheaval I have both experienced and caused since this unasked-for journey began, have all made me a bit gun-shy when it comes to being an official spokesperson for the Christian faith. So I shut down my old theological blog a couple of years ago (and quit contributing to others) and started a podcast called *Drunk Ex-Pastors* with my agnostic best friend, Christian, as a way to let my proverbial hair down a bit and dispel any lingering myths that I'm a holy person. I felt as though I had spent the majority of my life laboring under the burden of being this shining example of spiritual strength and certitude, and I just couldn't take it anymore. I wanted to just *be,* and to have the luxury of open-mindedness and the humility to admit that I don't know what the hell I'm talking about most of the time.

This is part of the reason why my "career" as a Catholic writer and speaker was so short-lived. Soon after I converted, I was interviewed on the popular Catholic TV program *The Journey Home* and spoke at a couple of large conferences, sharing the stage with some of my heroes of the Catholic faith. But as I looked down that road, I became increasingly unsettled. This was brought home to me one day while sitting and chatting with my priest, Fr. Kurt Nagel. I had just returned from Steubenville, Ohio, where I had spoken at Franciscan University's annual "Defending the Faith" conference, and he must have picked up on something about my demeanor, because he asked, "Jason, do you actually want to be a Catholic spokesman and public figure?" I hemmed and hawed a bit, but he kept pressing the issue. At that moment it occurred to me that I had never really taken the time to stop and consider that very simple question. I had been a public apologist for Protestantism my entire adult life, and now that I was Catholic, I had just assumed I would keep on being a mascot, only now for my new team. But what I never had the courtesy to ask myself was, "Is this what I want?" And when I did get around to asking that question, I realized to my surprise that the answer was no.

There was a problem, though. By the time I reached this place, I had already finished writing the first draft of this book! And believe me, that initial manuscript was very different from the volume you're holding in your hand (or reading on your screen) now. It was a perfectly fine manuscript, but it was much more polemical and technical and case-making than I was comfortable with, and by the time I finished it, I just felt kind of disgusted by the whole thing. The only solution I could think of was to try to put a stop to the whole project. I called Gary Jansen, my editor at Random House, and asked if we could just scrap this book altogether and do something else instead. After some persuasion, he agreed that we should take the project in a completely new direction, a direction that I felt good about. So we put our heads together, and *Misfit Faith* is the result. It's no longer really a "Catholic book" or a defense of my turning to Rome. Rather, it's an honest, heart-on-my-sleeve account of where I'm at, how I got here, and how, when I arrived, I found a lot of other misfits sitting around, drinking, and feeling a lot of the same emotions and struggles I'd been feeling. This book is a chronicle of my journey from one kind of faith to another. It's what happens when a person has reached the end of himself and the way he used to be (and the way he used to believe), and yet, despite being inundated with reasons to give up on everything, he just can't bring himself to walk away from the God that he doesn't even believe is there half the time. In short, *Misfit Faith* seeks to express in words the last gasp of those who feel like religious vagabonds and exiles with nowhere to really call home, who have realized that they will always, ever, and only be fans of spirituality rather than full-fledged members of the team. Echoing what I said above, a misfit trying to believe is a recipe for disaster. But if the gospel teaches us anything, it's that disaster is where grace happens.

I am under no illusion that everyone who reads this book will like it. (In fact, I can probably list a hundred people by name right now who I'm certain will hate it.) But part of the liberating process I have undergone since leaving the ministry is the freedom not to give a toss whether people like what I say or not. So there.

Jason Stellman
Snoqualmie, WA

1

Daddy Issues

(Or, Does God Deserve That "World's Best Father" Mug?)

"I Believe in God, the Father Almighty . . ."

When I was a missionary with Calvary Chapel in Europe, I was introduced to the work of the singer-songwriter Rich Mullins. I was initially dismissive of him because of how much I think Christian music sucks. I mean, there's only so much soft rock "Jesus Is My Boyfriend" drivel a guy can take, and I was at the point where if I heard one more song about how Jesus wants to take me into a garden and whisper sweet nothings into my ear with his hot breath while running his hand over the small of my back, I was going to light myself on fire. But the other missionaries (most of whom shared my disdain for religious rock) assured me that Mullins was different, and when I popped in the cassette tape of *A Liturgy, a Legacy, and a Ragamuffin Band*, I realized they were right. There was something very human and earthy about his style and his words, a grittiness to which I was unaccustomed, especially when juxtaposed with the glammy and overproduced Christian music that was popular at the time.

One of the songs on that album was called "Creed," and in it Mullins simply sang one of the oldest expressions of the Christian faith, the Apostles' Creed, the first line of which reads, "I believe in God, the Father Almighty, maker of heaven and earth." He then added a chorus, part of which said (in reference to the Creed), "I did not make it, no, it is making me." That particular line initially struck me as odd until I remembered the words of Paul in Romans 6, where the apostle referred to the gospel as "that form of doctrine *to which you were delivered*" (verse 17, NKJV). The idea is that the truth of God is not something over which man sits as judge or maker but rather something that makes and judges him. Faith is constantly sculpting us, is what I'm getting at.

As I made my own transition out of a rather high-strung and sure-of-myself Protestantism into a more unclenched, misfit Catholicism, I realized that what was "making" Rich Mullins, and what had made so many other saints down through the ages, was the truth contained in that first line of the Creed: "I believe in God, the Father Almighty." As elementary as it sounds, it was *the fatherhood of God* that began to play the most significant role in my own spiritual transformation, a transformation that left very few nerves untouched and very few stones unturned. What I'd like to do in this chapter is explore God's fatherhood, seeking to show how a better grasp of this reality can transform our view of God and our view of ourselves as his children.

"This My Son Was Dead, and Is Alive Again!"

The concept of "the fatherhood of God" may be unfamiliar to many of you, so let me explain it as best I can. Since around the fourth century, the Church has taught that God is three-in-one, that he exists in three distinct but coequal Persons: the Father, the Son, and the Holy Spirit. (And please don't try to actually *understand* this. It's weird, mysterious, and not really the kind of thing we can wrap our brains around.) This is why Jesus, when teaching about his Father, often resorted to stories and parables, and without a doubt, his parable of the prodigal son is one of the most illustrative portrayals of this idea in all of Scripture. In case you're not familiar, or your memory's a bit rusty, I'll sum it up:

The younger of two brothers decides that he wants his share of his father's inheritance immediately rather than waiting for his father to get around to actually dying. (Old people take forever to do anything, am I right?) The father agrees, and the younger son heads to a far-off land—whatever antiquity's version of Vegas was—in order to party, sleep with, umm, "women of ill repute," and engage in whatever other salacious activity money can buy. (Use your imagination. Actually, don't.) Not unpredictably, the son reaches the end of his rope once his inheritance is exhausted: he is living in squalor and tending swine, even finding himself so hungry that he would gladly have filled his belly with the scraps he was feeding his pigs. The prodigal finally comes to his senses and decides to humble himself and return to his father, even rehearsing a confession speech about his own unworthiness to be considered a son and willingness to be hired on as a servant. But before he can even reach his door, his father sees him afar off and runs to meet him. And despite the protestations of his older and better-behaved son, the father embraces the prodigal, kisses him, and before the younger son can deliver his mea culpa, his father commands that he be adorned as an honored member of the family and that a lavish feast be prepared to celebrate his return.

Now, speaking for myself, I can imagine a much more likely response to this son from his father upon hearing his son's initial request: "What's that? You want to skip the remainder of my life as well as the funeral and get straight to the reading of the will? And you want this so you can run off and dishonor yourself and me with a bunch of hookers and blow? Nice try, but howsabout instead I just write you out of my will altogether, you little punk?" But this father reacted very differently to his son's disloyalty, which is what is so obviously striking about the story. In spite of such willful disregard, the father responded to his son's selfish request and eventual return with utter grace, understanding, and familial love. In a word, he responded like a father.

What Is God, Really?

For most of my Christian life, ideas like "the Trinity" and "the fatherhood of God" were things I had little practical use for. They were concepts I kept in my back pocket in case some Mormons (who deny them) came knocking at my door: "Listen up: You guys are totally in a cult. Read these verses about how God is three-in-one and get back to me. And quit it with the whole polygamy thing. Geez." While God being a "Father" could become useful for apologetical purposes, it didn't make much difference in day-to-day life, is what I'm saying.

More often than not when I would present the gospel, I would root it in a God who was a creator and judge but not so much a Father. I'd say something like "The God who created all things, and who also made you, will one day be your judge when you stand before him on the last day," and so on. Not that there's anything wrong with that, of course, the Bible is clear that God acts as both creator and judge. But the question I began to ponder was, "Is being a creator, or being a judge, actually what makes God *God*? Are these traits necessary? Do they define him?" The answer is obviously no. We know this because before Genesis 1:1 happened, God was still God. He didn't somehow *need* to create anything in order to fully be who he is. This idea that God did not create out of some inherent need on his part flies in the face of the way the gospel is often presented: God is displayed as having been bored and in need of companionship before he created man, and therefore his creative efforts were to assuage his divine loneliness. In short, God had a man-shaped hole in his heart that only we could fill.

But if God would still be God if he never created anything, and if his godhood would not be diminished in the slightest if he never judged anyone, then what exactly, at the end of the day, is he? What is it that makes God *God*? The answer is simple (albeit hopelessly complex): God is three-in-one, he is a Father who has a Son, from both of whom proceeds the Holy Spirit. Three divine Persons, but one God. Because of this, there was never a "time" when God lacked companionship—the Father exists in a divine community with the Son and Spirit, and therefore there has ever been fellowship, communion, and love between the Persons of the Trinity from all eternity past. In other words, God, by definition, is never alone. And if he is never alone, he can never be lonely. Unlike those earthly fathers who wish they were still unattached and single, God the Father is like Clark Griswold in the *National Lampoon's Vacation* films: He's the consummate family man.

Family Matters and Deadbeat Baby-Daddies

Okay, so if what makes God *God* is not that he is a creator or a judge but a Father, the next question is, "What do fathers do? What makes them fathers?" The answer is obvious: What makes a father a father is that he has children, he produces offspring by imparting his essence and nature to them, reproducing his image in his sons and daughters.

How does this relate to God the Father? Well, to put it super simply, God is a Father because he has a Son.[1] How does this affect us? This is where things get interesting. If what makes God *God* is his being a Father, and if as a Father his role is to reproduce his image in his offspring, and if this paternal and familial relationship extends beyond heaven to earth, then this means that we, together with Jesus, are "children of God" and "partakers of the divine nature" (Rom. 8:14–17; 2 Pet. 1:4).

Now, you may just be rolling your eyes at how obvious and elementary this all is, and if so, I would ask you to kindly put your eyes back where they belong and stick with me. Salvation involves so much more than the standard deal of being forgiven of your sins and going to heaven when you die. In fact, once I started to think about my own

---

1. In the words of the Creed referred to above, a Catholic professes at every Mass that he believes in Jesus Christ, "the only-begotten Son of God, born of the Father before all ages . . . begotten, not made, consubstantial with the Father." Now, it would be easy to get bogged down in theological detail here, but I would prefer to avoid that. (You're welcome.) Suffice it to say that when the Creed says that Christ is not "made" but "begotten," it intends to convey that the Son was not created by God the way we were. No, he is (in the words of theologians way smarter than I) "eternally begotten," meaning that he has ever and always existed, but that existence has ever and always been as a Son whom the Father generates.

relationship with God in familial terms, it made mere forgiveness seem kind of paltry.

The expression of Christianity that I left behind certainly professed belief in the fatherhood of God. But as I
hinted at above, God-as-Father wasn't nearly as central as
he should have been, at least not for me. Nowhere was this
shortcoming more glaringly seen than in the way I used to
think about my own standing with God, especially in re-
lation to my sins (of which there were plenty). According
to my old mind-set, God was a strict lawgiver whose commands expressed the utter holiness of his character. Any
violation of those commands, then, was a sin against the
unbending justice of God's law, and as such, it demanded
eternal punishment. Stop and consider that idea for just a
moment. According to Christianity as understood through
my prior lenses, any breach—as the dogma goes, no matter
how slight or even accidental—causes infinite guilt in the
one committing the infraction. Yikes. Just from writing that,
I peed myself a little.

Let's tease out the ramifications of this God-as-lawgiver
model a bit, shall we? The story starts in the womb, where
you, through no actual fault of your own (obviously), are le-
gally charged with the guilt of Adam's original sin. So there
you are, a grain-of-rice-size zygote, repugnant and morally
odious in the sight of God due to the imputation to your account of the guilt of someone else's sin whom you've never
even met (because you're, like, a *fetus*). I know, right? That's
some pretty messed-up stuff right there, seemingly flying in

warmed up). Alrighty then, I'm off to work. Love you!" Now, I'm sure that someone defending the God-as-lawgiver paradigm would insist that God, unlike us, is never arbitrarily or unnecessarily strict, but rather is bound by his holiness to make the demands and issue the sentences that he does. (That's certainly what I would have said when I was operating from within this system.) But that just reinforces the point I was making above. If what makes him God is his being a Father rather than a creator, lawgiver, or judge, then shouldn't we expect that his divine fatherhood would come to the fore more often than we see it doing?

To put the question more directly, shouldn't I expect God to be a better father than I am? So to move from the lesser to the greater, if all earthly families illustrate divine fatherhood (Eph. 3:14–15), and if my love for my own children is more powerful than the rules I impose on them or my displeasure when they break them, then wouldn't it stand to reason that the same is not only true of the divine Father but infinitely more true of him?

World's Greatest Dad?

It has been observed that kids, and girls especially, take their cues for future relationships from their own fathers. Alanis Morissette sings about this poignantly in her song "Princes Familiar," which includes lines like "Papa, cry for your princess so that she will find gentle princes familiar,"

and "Papa, listen to your princess so that she will find atten-
tive princes familiar." I'm fortunate enough to have a father
who sacrificed a whole lot, including probably the best job in
the world (a sportswriter covering the Angels for the *Orange
County Register*), in order to be present for my brother and
me and to not miss out on our childhood. But I have known
a lot of people, most of them women, who didn't have this
privilege and who have had to overcome a lot of childhood
neglect in order to have healthy relationships now. Something inside all of us suggests that whatever else fatherhood
may entail, at the very least it involves a good measure of
presence, care, communication, and love.

This being the case, a huge question began to haunt me:
If God is a Father, is he any good at it? If God's overarching
purpose with respect to us is to *be what he is,* to father a family in whom he can reproduce his divine image, then how's
that working out for him? Will he be able to pull this whole
"fathering a worldwide family" stunt off? Call me an over-
simplifier, but I keep falling back on these basic ideas that a
Father is simply what God *is,* and that fathering a worldwide
family is simply what God *does.*[2] Sure, it's hardly original and

---

2. As God has always fathered his divine Son, so in Genesis the Father engages in the paternal act of "mak[ing] man in his image and
according to his likeness" (1:26), and Luke's genealogy of Christ
traces him back to "the son of Enos, the son of Seth, the son of
Adam, the *son of God*" (3:38). Mankind's first earthly father, then,
was himself a son of God, made in the image and according to the
likeness of his heavenly Father.

far from biblically sophisticated, but so what? We're misfits, remember? We'd rather find a bit of comfort in simple ideas even when being nontechnical means that no theological tradition can lay exclusive claim to us. So I'm quite content to affirm that yes, God knows a thing or two about fathering a family. And yeah, he's pretty good at it too.

Now, I didn't always see things this way or consider fatherhood the proper lens through which to see God. There was a time when I would draw comfort from those passages in the Bible that seem to highlight the sparseness of heaven's final population. (You know, "Narrow is the way that leads to life, and there are few who find it," and all that.) For some reason, the idea that heaven would be populated by, like, me and nine of my closest friends was pretty appealing. After all, we were the ones who *really* understood the gospel, right? But the broad evangelicals and Jehovah's Witnesses and papists? Puh-leeze. They're trusting in their good works, so hell serves them right.

But is this how we would expect the heavenly Father to behave? If I, as an earthly father, truly love my children with a deep paternal affection, wouldn't I do everything in my power to ensure that all my beloved offspring are cared for and safe for as long as I am able? For example, if one of my children expressed his affection for me in a way that was very different from the way my others did, and if the others resented this difference, wouldn't I as their loving father seek to bridge this divide, accept the unique way my son sought to love me, and insist that this child, no less than my others, would be guaranteed his share in my estate (paltry though that inheritance might be) once I pass from the scene? Would I really take sides in this kind of sibling rivalry, dismissing the love and honor that one of my kids offers me as illegitimate and unacceptable, despite his heartfelt sincerity in offering it?

Swinging from the natural to the spiritual, let's return to our rhetorical question posed above: "Is God as good at being a Father as I am?" The question is almost blasphemous, it is so ridiculous. If divine fatherhood is the archetype and my earthly fatherhood is but a copy, then any display of mercy or understanding that I might render to my earthly kids only pales compared to what my heavenly Father shows toward me. The conclusion that I have begun to draw from this is that God simply cannot be as jealous to protect the property values in heaven as I once thought he was, and that admitting the riffraff and ragamuffins, despite how pissed off it might make his "good kids," is exactly the kind of thing we would expect a Father par excellence to do. (And remember, in the parable with which we began this chapter, the prodigal's older and better-behaved brother was offended at how lavish his father was with his mercy and forgiveness, but his father basically told him to pipe down and get over himself.)

How far can we extend this idea? How broadly dare we apply this notion of God as a heavenly Father whose mercy knows no bounds? I can't help but think of the words of Paul, who said, "[I pray that you may grasp] what is the breadth and length and depth and height, and to know the love of Christ that surpasses knowledge, that you may be filled with all the fullness of God" (Eph. 3:18–19). If there were a limit to the love of God in Christ, the apostle certainly didn't know about it. In fact, he also wrote, "For as in Adam all die, so also in Christ shall all be made alive" (1 Cor. 15:22). Given the infinite scope of God's love, and given the fact that he is a more merciful Father than I am, does this mean I'm free to expect that his merciful salvation really will extend to "all," as Paul seems to suggest? And can it be that, when all is said and done, heaven will be fuller than even the most optimistic of us expected, and hell will be emptier than any of us dared hope?

Pagans, Atheists, and a Fatherly Response

Now, I know that for some people, even the bare suggestion that heaven's residents may outnumber hell's can ruffle feathers. I can hear the objection now: "There is no way heaven will be as populated as hell! Think of all the atheists and agnostics and Muslims and Europeans and liberals and Kardashians there have been throughout history! Surely none of them are going to make it past the pearly gates?" The idea here is that even if every single professing Christian makes it to heaven (to which our objector would certainly take issue, since most of them probably have bad theology or morals), those professing Christians still wouldn't equal the number of people who make no profession of faith in

Christ at all. And since both bad and non-Christians go to hell, Jesus doesn't really have much chance of winning the population game, does he?

Not so fast. If I, as an earthly father, were able to love my offspring with a love powerful enough to actually overcome their failure to love me as they should, then I surely would do so. Likewise, if, for some reason, one of my children didn't know that I was her father, and if she went through life either not knowing that her father was still alive or thinking that some other man besides me was her dad, I wouldn't consider her failure to acknowledge me as hatred or antipathy on her part but would know that it stemmed from ignorance and happenstance. I could never bring myself to respond to this with anger, punishment, and disinheritance. Rather, I would (as much as was in my power to do so) seek to overcome her lack of knowledge and shower her with the fatherly gifts that are hers by birthright.

Moving again from the natural to the supernatural realm, the fact is that God the Father, unlike us earthly fathers, does have the power to overcome any and all obstacles to his paternal love for his children whom he has created and marked with his heavenly imprint. In other words, despite my best efforts, one of my earthly children may resist my attempts to reach out and repair a damaged relationship, or (to use the example above) she may continue on in ignorance of her true paternity, never knowing who her real father is. But God is not limited the way we humans are, and he is therefore not bound by our human shortcomings at displaying fatherly devotion. He can melt the hardest heart and enlighten the most darkened mind, all by the mere exercise of his will, power, and love.

As you may have guessed, there is a fancy, technical term for the idea that some people are simply unaware of God, his existence, or his fatherly claim upon their lives (or perhaps they are aware of these things but are nevertheless sincerely unconvinced of them): *invincible ignorance.* Slightly insulting verbiage aside, what this means is that a person's failure to acknowledge God as his or her Father is not necessarily the result of sinful obstinacy or willful rebellion. The person may just be unaware or unconvinced of God's divine fatherhood. An example of the former would be people who, through no fault of their own, were born in a part of the world where a different religion from Christianity is practiced and a different god from "the Father of our Lord Jesus Christ" is worshipped. Now, if the God of the Creed really is "the Father Almighty," would he be able to reach even those who don't know about him with his merciful and paternal love? The answer is easy: yes. The harder question for some Christians is "He *can,* but *will* he?" In other words, just because God is able to do something, does this mean he is necessarily willing to do it? When taken in the abstract, the answer is obviously no. God's secret will is just that: secret and inscrutable, and we cannot presume to know that he *will* do something merely because he *can.* But does the redemption of humankind fall into this category? Is the adoption of sons and daughters from every kindred, tongue, tribe, and nation really the kind of thing we simply cannot know whether God is, like, into doing? Has he really left us in the dark regarding his saving intentions for fallen sons and daughters of Adam?

I would echo Scripture and argue that no, God has not left us wondering whether he wills to save all people. In addition to Paul's statement cited above about how "in Christ all shall be made alive," we read in 1 Timothy 2:3–4 that "God our Savior . . . desires all people to be saved and to come to the knowledge of the truth." And in 2 Peter 3:9, "The Lord is not slow to fulfill his promise as some count slowness, but is patient toward you, not wishing that any should perish, but that all should reach repentance." It is clear that when it comes to God's will and desire, his choice is that all people be saved. And if you think about it, this is pretty unsurprising since, after all, he is a Father. I mean (as I said above), if I had a bunch of kids, I would want them all to share in my earthly estate when they came of age, regardless of whether they were good and obedient children.

The issue, then, comes down to whether God will actually *accomplish* what he clearly says he *desires* to accomplish. This is where my newfound appreciation for the fatherhood of God comes in. I know this may sound overly simplistic, but I have come to think that if God is a Father by nature, and if that fatherhood compels him both to sire offspring and to desire that all of them come to participate fully and finally in his eternal inheritance, then he will do whatever he must to see this loving and paternal will comes to pass. Will he let the fact that some of us are born in non-Western or non-Christian countries stand in his way or thwart his divine will? Well, I wouldn't if I had the ability to see my plans to fruition, and I'm not a fraction as loving a father as God is!

A powerful example of invincible ignorance being conquered by divine love can be found in the volume from C. S. Lewis's *The Chronicles of Narnia* titled *The Last Battle*. The character Emeth is at the point of death and realizes that he has been worshipping the false god, Tash, his entire life (rather than the lion Aslan, a figure of Christ). Here is how Lewis describes the encounter between this "pagan" and Aslan the lion:

> The Glorious One bent down his golden head and touched my forehead with his tongue and said, "Son, thou art welcome." But I said, "Alas, Lord, I am no son of thine but the servant of Tash." He answered, "Child, all the service thou hast done to Tash, I account as service done to me."
>
> But I said also (for the truth constrained me), "Yet I have been seeking Tash all my days." "Beloved," said the Glorious One, "unless thy desire had been for me thou shouldst not have sought so long and so truly. For all find what they truly seek."[3]

I remember being more than just a tad scandalized when I first read this in my twenties: "Wait, what? This (presumably swarthy) guy Emeth, who'd been serving some

---

3. C. S. Lewis, *The Last Battle* (London: Bodley Head, 1956).

Narnia-version of Allah or whatever all his life, gets to go to Narnia-heaven simply because he was sincere and devout? What's up with that?" But this objection stemmed from an unfamiliarity with the (very Catholic) idea that grace doesn't overturn nature but builds upon and perfects it. (More on this later on.) In other words, the way God works is not to undo or subvert our natural way of thinking, but to beautify it and place an exclamation point after all true human ideas. If an earthly father would accept the genuine yet misdirected attempts of his child to honor him, then it follows that our heavenly Father would be even more willing to do so (since it isn't anyone's fault where they were born or which religious tradition they were reared in, and therefore it's not exactly fair to punish them or hold them accountable for something beyond their control, especially when "hold them accountable" means waterboarding them for all eternity).

A similar case can be made on behalf of the sincere agnostic or atheist. Now, I'm sure there are plenty of atheists and agnostics out there who are in it only for the sinning. ("Hey, I decided I like sex and drugs, so I suddenly don't believe in God anymore. How convenient!") But to be honest, I don't know many of them. To the contrary, most of the ones I know are genuinely unconvinced—or genuinely no longer convinced—of the Christian narrative. Moreover, many of them aren't exactly living lives of deviant debauchery that their atheism or agnosticism sanctions, but are living pretty normal lives that wouldn't require much repentance if they were to convert or revert to Christianity. So what are we to think about these people? The thought of dismissing them as liars who say they don't believe in God when in reality they just don't like him, or of insisting that they submit to God despite their unbelief, doesn't sound very charitable or love-your-neighbor-ish. Neither does biting the bullet and hoping God punishes them for being honest and not violating their own consciences by worshipping a God they don't think is really there.

More important, how should God the Father think of them? The notion that his jealousy for his own glory should eclipse his love for his creation doesn't strike me as particularly paternal, and insisting that he should be sufficiently offended at not being worshipped enough to consign the bulk of humanity to everlasting torment just to prove a point sounds downright sinister. Now, a few years ago I would have insisted that the numerical disparity between heaven and hell—the latter being way more populated than the former—serves to illustrate just how gracious God is to his chosen few. Like a judge granting one man in a thousand a judicial pardon would make that single pardon appear incredibly rare and valuable, so, according to my line of thinking, God's frugality with his grace is what protects the preciousness of its worth. After all, if our divine lawgiver and judge were to be too indiscriminate with his acquittals or lavish with his pardons, those gifts might start to feel cheap and easy to come by. But if what makes God *God* is being not a lawgiver or a judge but a Father, this whole line of thinking immediately begins to unravel. While lawgivers insist on being heeded and judges need to inspire fear and respect, fathers don't focus as much on those issues as they do on loving their children and pulling out all the stops to ensure their safety and well-being. Should we expect anything less from our heavenly Father than we do from earthly ones? While none of us knows the eternal fate of anyone's soul, is it really beyond the realm of possibility that "God the Father Almighty" would exercise his loving power to soften the heart and enlighten the mind of even the most ardent atheist? After all, I'm quite certain that even the most prideful among God's detractors would be happy to be proven wrong if the alternative were suffering eternal torment in a lake of fire.

A final word to those who may be reading these words with a measure of skepticism: I get it. Really. And I don't begrudge you your furrowed brow and head scratching. My only question to you is this: Do you *want* what I'm saying to be true? Do you hope that God's fatherhood will eventually result in hell's being virtually or completely empty? I'm not asking if you *believe* this to be the case but if you sincerely *desire* it to be. Why would I ask such a thing? Unfortunately, the lenses through which many Christians see the world are such that the opening wide of heaven's gates to any and all represents a threat to those whose doctrinal precision sort of earns them a spot. In a kind of perverse example of spiritual "white flight," when people with the wrong theological skin color (or no theology at all) are given prime heavenly real estate, it drives down property values and ruins all the fun. I mean, what's so special about heaven if everyone gets a ticket?

But for those who have come to not just assent to the fatherhood of God but to truly bask in and embrace it, the bigger and more diverse the divine family, the better. The fuller the eternal kingdom, the better. The emptier hell, the better. And any set of biblical or theological lenses that suggest otherwise should be swapped out immediately and traded for ones that enable the universal saving plan of the Father to be on full display.

2

Matter Matters

(Or, How Grace Perfects Nature)

Micturated-Upon Rugs and Central Dogmas

In *The Big Lebowski* (one of my all-time favorite movies), the weed- and White Russian–addled protagonist, Jeff "the Dude" Lebowski, comes home from grocery shopping and is assaulted by two thugs who demand that he repay the money that his wife owes to their gangster boss. The problem, the Dude explains, is that he is not married, and that they've got the wrong Jeffrey Lebowski. The thugs realize their mistake, and in a moment of frustration, one of them proceeds to urinate on the Dude's rug before they leave. This was no ordinary or easily forgivable transgression since, as the Dude repeatedly remarks, "That rug really tied the room together." Heeding the advice of a friend, the Dude proceeds to track down the thugs' intended target and, since he's a millionaire, demand that he give him a new rug for his apartment.

(The wealthy Lebowski's reply is priceless: "I just want to understand this: Every time a rug is micturated upon in this fair city, I have to compensate the person?") One thing leads to another, and hilarity ensues. You should totally watch it.

While some theologians are uncomfortable with the idea that Christianity has a "central dogma," few would balk at the notion that if there is a fundamental core to the faith, it is the coming-in-the-flesh of the Son of God. In short, all that stuff we celebrate at Christmas? It really ties the room together. What I'd like to do in this chapter is show how the coming-in-the-flesh (or Incarnation) of the Son of God "ties everything together" by giving us a pattern for what to expect when heaven touches earth. If Jesus is our concrete exemplar, then how his "God-ness" affected his "man-ness" sets the stage for how grace and nature intersect across the board, in all areas. And trust me, the practical payoff from all this is massive: How we relate to those who don't share our beliefs, what kinds of music and media we allow ourselves to consume, and how we engage with hot-button topics like the environment, abortion, and gun control are all profoundly affected by what we think about Jesus, and especially how his divinity and humanity relate to each other. So stay tuned, and hang on to your seats!

Plenty of ink has been spilled attempting to describe the mystery of the coming of Christ in the flesh.[1] But in

---

1. Here's a good attempt: "The Son of God assumed human nature and became man in order to accomplish our salvation in that same

the interests of keeping the most complex thing ever super simple, suffice it to say that Jesus was not 50 percent God and 50 percent man, that his human body was not indwelt with a divine soul at some point during his life, and that he was not a divine Person and a human at one and the same time. No, the Son is a divine Person who assumed a human nature, and *his divinity did not swallow up or eclipse his humanity but elevated and perfected it.*

Okay, so why is this important? Well, if God becoming human is the central hub from which everything else about the Christian faith flows, then it follows that properly understanding the relationship of Christ's divinity to his humanity is important for grasping how heaven and earth intersect, and how God relates to us as individuals. Like, imagine if Jesus of Nazareth was some human carpenter guy cruising around Galilee when out of nowhere (*bam!*) he was taken over by a God-virus and became a kind of hybrid zombie whose will and actions were now commandeered by a higher power that he couldn't control. If this were the case, then a couple of conclusions would follow. First, it would give us a pattern according to which God, when he intervenes in human history and with us as individuals, does so in a way that is weird and unnatural and even violent, as though

---

human nature. Jesus Christ, the Son of God, the second Person of the Trinity, is both true God and true man, not part God and part man." Catholic Church, *Catechism of the Catholic Church,* 2nd ed. (Washington, DC: United States Catholic Conference, 2000), p. 883.

at any moment we might go into a freaky seizure, and our eyes would glass over, and our humanity would be bypassed so that divinity could take over and assume control of us against our will (which is exactly the impression I get when I watch what faith healers do to people on TV). Second and more broadly, this scenario would give the impression that spiritual concerns sort of run roughshod over temporal ones and that heaven can merely trump earth with an air of dismissal. But the thing is, I like earth way too much to let it be treated in that kind of "Who's your daddy?" manner. And it turns out God does too.

What I have been discovering over the past several years—and what all believers would benefit from discovering as well—is a way to think about this God-in-the-flesh thing that can be applied to the way I think about life more broadly. We need to see *grace* (by which I mean all the eternal, heavenly stuff) as not destroying or devaluing but as legitimizing and perfecting *nature* (by which I mean all the temporal, earthly stuff). This connection was largely lost on me during my sure-of-myself evangelical days. Yeah, I could've articulated correct beliefs about Jesus, but the way I often thought about and treated earth and its material concerns was inconsistent with those proper Jesus-beliefs that I claimed to embrace. For example, I would often be very dismissive of, say, cultural self-help gurus like Oprah and Tony Robbins because, after all, they're not even Christians, so what real help or counsel could they possibly have to offer? The assumption in that kind of thinking was that earth is at odds with heaven, and heaven is just waiting for earth to shut up so that it can start talking. (More on this in a moment.)

There is a bit of irony here: I wanted to make Jesus "relevant" to nonbelievers by showing that he could fix all their problems and heal their brokenness (which is obviously important), but I completely missed the fact that divinity clothing himself in humanity is itself the most relevant thing God could have ever done. Don't get me wrong, we could all use divine tips on balancing our checkbooks or "raising positive kids in a negative world," but that's sort of like missing the forest for the trees. In Christ, God married himself to human nature in such a way as to raise humanity to the level of (small-G) gods ourselves! Because of the Son's Incarnation, crucifixion, resurrection, and ascension to heaven (you know, all the stuff we celebrate at Christmas and Easter), we humans actually share in the divine life of the Trinity! God is our Father and Christ is our Brother! These lofty mysteries, far from being clinical and dusty ideas suitable only for ivory-tower scholars or cave-dwelling mystics to ponder, are what actually make possible all that practically relevant other stuff we long for. In short, the whole reason God can help you with the day-to-day difficulties of life is *because* he is invested in earth and in humanity, so much so that he entered into these realities in Christ.

So how does this apply to us and the challenges we face practically? What does all this Jesus-in-the-flesh stuff mean for misfits like us who spend most of our time without a spiritual clue? Great question! Let's roll up our sleeves and dive in.

A Divine Yes to Humanity

"Grace perfects nature." In many ways, this formula captures the essence of the Christian faith. Once we understand that the Son's taking of a human nature and human flesh did not destroy, eclipse, or undermine humanity but elevated and eventually glorified it, the closer we'll get to actually applying the Incarnation to our own daily lives.

As I alluded to above, in my younger days I saw earth and its material concerns as threatening and worthy of suspicion. I would say things like "You shouldn't watch that—it's *of the world*" or "I wouldn't listen to that—it's completely *worldly*" or "Don't pay attention to him—he just has the wisdom *of the world*." To be fair, this fear of anything "worldly" comes primarily from a passage in the Bible, 1 John 2:15–16, which says: "Do not love the world or the things in the world. If anyone loves the world, the love of the Father is not in him. For all that is in the world—the desires of the flesh and the desires of the eyes and pride of life—is not from the Father but is from the world." Now, the most famous passage in all of Scripture (also written by John) begins with the phrase "For God so *loved the world*" (John 3:16), so it's clear that some defining of terms is in order. After all, it's pretty irrational to say that in John 3 God is violating his command in

1 John 2. What, then, is meant by "the world" and our being forbidden to love it?

As I mentioned above, many believers assume a posture of immediate mistrust of "the world," and by "the world" they mean anything that is not spiritual. "Spiritual" in such cases is often contrasted with "material," meaning that it is considered wrong or "carnal" to be overly concerned with physical and material things. For example, when I was a senior at Calvary Chapel High School in southern California, I, along with my fellow soon-to-be-graduates, faced the pressing question of what to do after high school. Many of my classmates were contemplating which college to attend, but to me such a path seemed "worldly" and "of the flesh." "If Jesus is coming back soon, and probably within the next decade," I reasoned, "what's the point in studying law or computers or medicine? All that material stuff won't matter up in heaven anyway!" Yep, *I said that*. And to this day my bank account balance serves as a constant reminder of my refusal to pursue any of these avenues. (I chose to move to Africa and be a missionary instead, which provided its own source of riches—just not the kind that pays the bills.)

Now, I hope you can see the fundamental error in this way of thinking. (And like most errors, it's ultimately a mistake about Jesus.) A couple of underlying assumptions here that are doing most of the heavy lifting are deeply flawed.

The first assumption is that matter and flesh are bad, which is why such things are contrasted to spiritual, heavenly things. The problem here is that, last I checked, the

Christian faith teaches that Jesus rose again *in the flesh*. As the Creed says, the same Lord Jesus Christ who "was incarnate of the Virgin Mary and became man" also "rose again on the third day . . . [and] ascended into heaven." If flesh-and-blood material things are bad, then apparently Jesus never got the memo, since he both rose bodily and ascended in the flesh to heaven. While it's true that Christ's risen body was a glorified body in many ways different from his previous one, it was a body nonetheless. To be dismissive or suspicious of material things simply because they're material is deeply mistaken, as though Jesus rose again as some kind of phantom, and as though the age to come will be some ethereal Twilight Zone where we float from cloud to cloud playing harps. But the risen Christ dispelled this idea when he appeared to his frightened disciples, saying, "Why are you troubled, and why do doubts arise in your hearts? See my hands and my feet, that it is I myself. Touch me, and see. For a spirit does not have flesh and bones as you see that I have" (Luke 24:38–39). And then to make sure they understood that he was not a ghost, he ate a plate of fish and chips right in front of them.

The other implicit assumption in this suspicious posture toward "worldly" pursuits is that heaven's aim is to necessarily thwart such things, as though divinity's role is to crush or frustrate humanity. But like the view that "spiritual" is the opposite of "physical," this is also a Jesus-error. Did Christ's divinity crush *his* humanity? Was some internal war being waged between the two natures of Jesus? Did his God-ness put his human-ness into a headlock and give it a noogie to show it who's boss? These questions are rhetorical, and their answer is obviously no. So continuing our move from the greater to the lesser, if divinity does not frustrate humanity in the case of Christ and his work of redemption, then it doesn't do it in our cultural endeavors either. In short, there is nothing inherently evil about physical things, and by pitting humanity against divinity, we will inevitably muck up the Incarnation and in so doing screw up everything else along with it. In a word, matter matters. As Adam Sandler's character in *The Wedding Singer* so poignantly reminded us, "We're living in a material world and I am a material girl . . . or boy." My point? As with Jesus, so with us. If his humanity was not an obstacle to redemption but the vehicle for it, then we have no cause to apologize for ours either. We ought rather to embrace and celebrate it.

"Christian" Art

From fourth grade on, I have been a big fan of music. My early tastes were pretty eclectic—I mean, when you're ten years old, you don't yet understand that certain genres of music don't mix very well with others. (Hence my being a fan of metal *and* hip-hop, of Mötley Crüe *and* Grandmaster Flash.) But music has always been a huge part of my life. I distinctly remember being in my kitchen listening to KROQ 106.7 and hearing U2's "New Year's Day" for the first time.

I begged my mom to drive me to the local record shop to buy their album *War,* and I was hooked (still am). Plus, since we were a nominally Christian family, and since Bono sang about Jesus sometimes, I figured God was pretty stoked that I was listening to "his kind of music" (which Mötley Crüe certainly was not!). I even sewed a big U2 *War* patch on the back of my bitchin' Quiksilver denim jacket.

You can imagine my surprise, therefore, when as a new student at Calvary Chapel High School, I was scolded for the patch. "You can't wear *that* to school," I was told by a teacher. "They're *secular.*" (The label was spoken in a kind of nervous hush, the way your grandma would have said, "They're nice people, even though they're *Jewish.*") When I tried to explain how Bono sings about Jesus sometimes, she wouldn't have any of it. U2's music was on a secular record label, and therefore U2 was secular, regardless of what Bono sang about. (If I had known that the album's closing track, "40," was actually Psalm 40 recited verbatim, I would have mentioned it, but I clearly didn't know enough Bible yet to point that out. And something tells me it wouldn't've mattered.)

You see, the mind-set into which I was being indoctrinated insisted that anything not explicitly religious is secular, and that anything secular is evil (all of which is based on the idea that spiritual things and physical ones are antithetical and diametrically opposed, the very Christological mistake we've been discussing). When it comes to something like music, the implicit—and more often explicit—

expectation is that no one who truly loves God and desires spiritual growth would ever listen to secular music, since the latter impedes the former (because, you know, grace frustrates nature). Since (according to this mentality) divinity and humanity have absolutely nothing in common, what possible spiritual good can come from earthly and physical things like listening to secular music or watching other forms of worldly media? Unless "Jesus" or "God" is mentioned explicitly (and nonblasphemously), the content is of little spiritual value and may in fact be spiritually harmful.

But as I've been insisting, if the eternal Son of God assumed a human nature and human flesh, and then died, rose, and ascended into heaven in that (now glorified) human nature and human flesh—all for the purpose of ushering humanity into the mutual fellowship and worship of the Holy Trinity—then not only is it incorrect to say that divinity and humanity have nothing in common, but saying that the two "have something in common" is an understatement akin to "Shaquille O'Neal is large." On the natural level, while I might have something in common with my younger brother (say, our shared love of the Lakers), that mutual interest is still something outside us. It is truer to say, not that I *have* something in common with some people, but that I *am* something in common with all people, since we all share in human nature. Transitioning from the natural to the spiritual level, the idea that I am one with my fellow humans because of our shared human nature is no truer than the idea that I am one with God because of my participation in the divine nature (2 Pet. 1:4). Because Christ's humanity is exalted, all human nature is now exalted. And because of the Son's having both human and divine nature, humanity is now forever in common with, and sharing in, divinity. That's why the New Testament calls him our forerunner (Heb. 6:20): As with Christ, so with his people, and where he goes, we follow.

The practical ramifications are endless. When it comes to music, recognizing the fact that musicians/lyricists are "only human" (as the unfortunate saying goes), far from disqualifying them from speaking meaningfully into the life of a believer, actually qualifies them for the task. Again, this is because receiving heavenly grace does not force upon us an entirely new operating system or delete everything from our human hard drive but affirms all the good stuff that we have downloaded previously (even providing the occasional update when necessary). I'm reminded of G. K. Chesterton's response to those who would seek to dismiss the Church's liturgical feasts and festivals due to their being of pagan origin: "They might as well say that our legs are of pagan origin. Nobody ever disputed that humanity was human before it was Christian; and no Church manufactured the legs with which men walked or danced, either in a pilgrimage or a ballet."[2] To put it another way, "Christian ideas and practices resemble pagan human ones? No shit." After all, God cre-

---

2. G. K. Chesterton, "The Story of Divorce," in *The Collected Works of G. K. Chesterton* (San Francisco: Ignatius Press, 1987), p. 4:264.

ated human nature, and Jesus shares in it to this very day, so when an artist who is in touch with his or her humanity captures what I happen to be feeling in a given moment, far from being shocking or looking upon it as an aberration or stroke of luck, it should be exactly the kind of thing we expect.

The same can be said of cinema. Despite the fundamentalists' insistence that believers watch only films with a PG rating (or better, avoid films altogether), the fact is that a good movie can tap into the deepest and most human recesses of our souls. And there is no reason to be surprised or embarrassed when a film "gets" you—the director who made it and the screenwriter who penned it are (gasp!) also human, and since they participate in your nature, why wouldn't they touch upon themes that we all share in common? Speaking personally, there are several films that I find myself returning to for this very reason. Some that come to mind are Richard Linklater's *Before Sunrise, Before Sunset,* and *Before Midnight* trilogy, as well as *The Perks of Being a Wallflower, Garden State,* and *Vicky Cristina Barcelona.* Since I'm something of a masochist, there are times when I'm feeling a bit down and want to make it worse, and these movies do the trick. I feel absolutely no guilt or shame for loving these secular expressions of art, much as I felt no shame for wearing my U2 jacket in high school. And as far as I'm concerned, anyone who would seek to instill that shame in me or shackle me with feelings of guilt simply doesn't have the interests of God in mind. After all, God is my Father, and shaming kids for being human just isn't the kind of thing good fathers do.

A Few Hot-Button Issues

This same principle of grace building upon and perfecting nature (and the common ground we share with all humanity due to the Incarnation) can also really help when certain hot-button issues arise. Take the ever-divisive issue of climate change (which Pope Francis addressed in an encyclical not long ago). The response on the part of my more conservative friends has been pretty uniform: "Wait, what? The pope believes in man-made climate change, and that we should be better stewards of our planet? But that's what all those liberals believe! And they want to murder our unborn kids, and the ones that slip through their nets, they'll just force to be cross-dressers!" The underlying idea here is that anything advocated by one's cultural/political opponents cannot be tolerated. I mean, they're our enemies, right? Why would we side with them?

But if all those shady liberals are also humans who share the same human nature that Christ and his people have, then perhaps they're not ultimately enemies after all. And if it's true that grace builds upon and perfects nature, then maybe the position of those who would seek to protect the environment need not be seen as hostile or antithetical to what believers ought to think about the matter? Going back to the theological errors discussed above, since it is wrong to think of the Son's divinity as canceling out or contradicting his humanity, it is therefore also wrong to think that God's wisdom on the matter of climate change and proper stewardship of our planet must necessarily contradict the recommendations of climate scientists and secular thought more broadly. Sure, maybe the broad scientific consensus on this issue is incorrect, but it is not *necessarily* incorrect simply because those who hold to it don't have Jesus-fish bumper stickers on their cars.

A similar line of reasoning can be used regarding the thorny issue of evolution and of origins in general. I have known many Christians who were raised to think that not only is evolution of any kind false but that any theory that denies a six-thousand-year-old earth is a betrayal of the biblical message. The result is not hard to predict: This person goes to university only to hear that he has been wrong about our planet's age, and since he has been brainwashed to think that the issue of origins is bundled together with the rest of Christianity as a kind of package deal, he ends up dismissing the whole thing as mere superstition or myth. Again, this fatal mistake stems from the false idea that science is not to be trusted since its source is secular. But if our proverbial prodigal had a more robust understanding of who Christ is and how he relates to us and our world, he would have understood that Christians don't need to look upon scientific theories as threats simply because they don't echo the Bible. (In fact, speaking to supernatural things isn't even science's job in the first place. That's what religion is for.) Rather, we can appreciate science for its contributions to our understanding of the physical world, even as we recognize its limitations regarding the metaphysical world.

Another hot-button issue is gun control, a topic that is debated whenever atrocities like Columbine, Sandy Hook, and Orlando occur. Whenever such a tragedy happens, certain media outlets warn us against "politicizing" the tragedy by having a discussion about reasonable gun legislation. "The bodies are still warm," we hear. "Now is not the time to talk about gun control." While this book is certainly not the place to debate the issue, what is relevant for our purposes is the fact that, lying beneath this fear of gun control on the part of many religious people is the notion that those who advocate sensible Second Amendment restrictions are secular thinkers. To be more specific, those who think we should have stricter gun control laws are the very ones who also advocate pro-choice politics and gay rights, and since those liberal positions are antithetical to conservative Christianity, we should refuse to entertain any of their ideas simply on principle.

The problem here is similar to the responses to climate change and evolution. Because the sources of most calls for gun control are secular, and because anything secular is supposedly antithetical to anything religious, we must strike a posture of fear and look upon all such ideas as threats to our faith. But if heaven and earth are not at war (since Christ's divinity and humanity are not at war), then we can discuss and evaluate "liberal" or secular ideas on their own merits without having to first make sure they pass the Jesus test.

To sum up, as long as I, as an evangelical Protestant, assumed a stance of suspicion toward all things worldly, I unwittingly displayed a heretical Christology and acted like a complete elitist douche. I implicitly pitted Christ's divinity against his humanity and explicitly pitted myself against all those unclean pagans out there, neither of which was healthy for my soul. But when I gained a better grasp of the fact that Jesus's incarnation brings humanity into fellowship with divinity, I became able to see myself in common with my fellow men and women, regardless of whether they shared my faith.

A Naturally Supernatural Gospel

One further aspect of this topic deserves mention here. As a Protestant who understood God's ways to be largely antithetical to man's, my view of the gospel message was that it virtually contradicted not only our natural way of thinking but every single other religion out there. "Mormons? Muslims? Catholics? Jews? They're pretty much all the same," I would have insisted. "They're trying to earn their ticket to heaven, whereas we faithful Protestants are unique in teaching that heaven can't be earned but must be received as a gift of grace alone."

While it is true that the grace of the gospel message is amazing (we have a song about it, after all), does it really overturn all of man's natural assumptions about how to find favor with God? According to countless religions since the dawn of time, the way to gain divine favor is to please God by doing works of mercy and sacrifice (in a word, by loving God and neighbor). Whether we're talking about a native American medicine man, a poor Tibetan monk, an enlightened Eastern guru, or a wealthy New England Episcopalian, at the end of the day each one is hoping to please whatever deity he or she worships by acts of love and compassion. As a good Protestant, I would have dismissed all this with a wave of the hand and a "You're *way* off," smugly delivered. "All those attempts to gain divine favor by loving God and neighbor are the exact opposite of the true gospel message," I would have insisted. "The real gospel is utterly counterintuitive to the way we naturally think!"

But if Jesus intended to undo all this please-the-Father-by-loving-God-and-neighbor business, he gave the exact opposite impression, saying things like "Love the Lord your God, and love your neighbor as yourself. This is the fulfillment of the law." (To be sure, the *how* of it all comes as quite a shock, which was Paul's point in 1 Corinthians 1:25 when he contrasted the "foolishness of God" and the "wisdom of men," but the *what* of it all is exactly what was expected.) The message of the gospel does not overturn our natural expectations about how to be saved—it reinforces them. Human beings intuitively operate under the impression that God is (or the gods are) pleased by our devotion, service, and love. This impression is correct. The gospel, far from saying "And now for something completely different," comes in and says "You are right—God is pleased by your devotion, service, and love. And here's how you can offer him those things." As Paul explained to the Romans, "What your own efforts couldn't get done, God did in Christ by the Spirit" (8:1–4, my paraphrase). In other words, God has made a way to accomplish what our natural way of thinking assumed—he didn't call that thinking into question and dismiss it altogether.

False Gods and False Devils

G. K. Chesterton once remarked that most of mankind can be placed into one of two groups: puritans (who make good things look bad) and pagans (who make bad things look good). The problem with both, Chesterton suggested, is that they lack the common sense needed to put pleasure in its proper place, with one side demonizing it and the other deifying it. Let's focus on the puritan: Perched on his shoulder (or for our purposes, on the fundamentalist's shoulder) is a little "angel" ever whispering about how evil the secular world is. The problem with this, as Chesterton pointed out, is that idolatry is not just the setting-up of false gods—it can also be the setting-up of false devils. "Sin is in a man's soul," he wrote, "not in his tools or toys."[3] If the Incarnation of the Son of God teaches us anything, it is that there is no longer any excuse for vilifying the physical world or labeling it evil as such.

This realization came as such a breath of fresh air for me, because I have always been a rather indulgent person when it comes to my pleasures. (Was it Oscar Wilde who said, "You can take away my necessities, but don't you dare touch my luxuries"?) I love good ale—IPAs in the summer and stouts in the winter—as well as espresso, bourbon, and Islay single malts. I like well-positioned candles, wainscoting and crown molding, wrought iron, and gargoyles on stain-glassed cathedrals. And cobblestones—don't forget the cobblestones. Rediscovering the Incarnation helped me embrace the richness of earth instead of repudiating it as "carnal" or "worldly." In short, my pleasures are not false gods, but they aren't false devils either. What I long for is a kind of earthy Christianity that does not merely hold its nose and begrudgingly make peace with the culture but embraces it, and its legitimate pleasures, with open arms, thanksgiving, and wonder. "Drink," Chesterton urged, "because you are happy, but never because you are miserable."[4]

---

3. *"Puritans and Pagans,"* in Dale Ahlquist, ed., *Common Sense 101: Lessons from G. K. Chesterton* (San Francisco: Ignatius Press, 2006), p. 178.

4. Ibid., pp. 178–79.

If we are to strike the proper balance between paganism and puritanism, we must sincerely wrestle with the possibility that, in our desire to avoid what the Bible calls "worldliness," we have mislabeled even the legitimate, earthly blessings of God as "secular" or "carnal." Having rid ourselves of the bathwater, we've tossed out the baby as well.

When it comes to embracing a Christianity that reflects the Incarnation by validating the physical world rather than vilifying it, perhaps the first step is recognizing that a true saint should be much more soiled than sanctimonious. With all due respect to medieval Catholic art, the halo-crowned mystic whose eyes gaze heavenward, whose mind seems impregnable by earthly worries, is hardly what comes to mind when I think about Jesus (the Jesus of the Gospels, I mean). He wept, got hungry, grew weary, got pissed off at people, and basically ran around being a complete pain in the ass to the religious establishment of his day. And I can't help but think that those of us who claim to admire him would do well to follow this example a bit more than we do. "Head in heaven, fingers in the mire" in the words of one poet,[5] "The face of a sinner, but the hands of a priest" in the words of another.[6]

To sum up, the coming-in-the-flesh of the second Person of the Trinity utterly precludes both the deifying *and* the

5. This line is from U2's "So Cruel" from their 1991 album *Achtung Baby*.
6. This line is from Sting's "Moon over Bourbon Street" from his 1985 album *The Dream of the Blue Turtles*.

demonizing of the earthly and physical world. Further, the ascension of Christ in his glorified humanity into heaven means that God, far from looking askance upon human nature, actually places a divine exclamation point after every true and beautiful expression of genuine humanness. God was smuggled into the world on Christmas morning, and the world was brought into heaven on Ascension Sunday. Perhaps the danger for many of us, then, is not that we enjoy earth too much but that we enjoy it too little.

3

Love, Not Law
(Or, Taking Our First Step into a Larger World)

The Familial Ties that Bind

I loved 1980s sitcoms growing up. I still do, actually. If you're old enough, you'll remember that these TV programs were very safe and family-oriented—you'd never see a woman stab another woman in the back of the head with a fork like on *Sons of Anarchy,* or witness a guy get sodomized with a pool cue like on *The Sopranos.* No, the only serious fare we'd get back then was the proverbial "hard-hitting episodes," like when college-age Natalie on *The Facts of Life* decided to have sex with her boyfriend (aptly named Snake), or when Arnold and Dudley on *Diff'rent Strokes* got molested by that creepy bike shop owner, or when Alex on *Family Ties* got hooked on meth because he had that big exam coming up. (Only someone like Alex P. Keaton would take drugs in order to *study.*) These shows presented a very sterilized view of life, one that assured us that while the world don't move to the beat of just one drum and never seems to be livin' up to our dreams, there ain't no nothin' we can't love each other through. Sha la la la.[1]

As a misfit, I know deep down that any version of Christianity that emphasizes the courtroom over the family room leaves me pretty much hopeless and screwed. My guess is that you agree. As much as we may mock those 1980s TV shows and their quaint family values, we need a Father rather than a judge, and it's in love rather than in law that we can truly find peace. This is why my faith has ceased to center upon mere contractual obligations, legal arrangements, and clinical exchanges of goods and services (such as "God, the divine and holy lawgiver, will forensically acquit you and render a not-guilty verdict in the courtroom of heaven") and focuses now on the familial exchange of *persons*. Statements like "That is yours, and this is mine" were transformed into "I am yours, and you are mine." Or, to invoke the words of Jesus: "[I pray] that they may all be one, just as you, Father, are in me, and I in you, that they also may be in us, so that the world may believe that you have sent me. The glory that you have given me I have given to them, that they may be one even as we are one, I in them and you in me, that they may become perfectly one, so that the world may know that you sent me and loved them even as you loved me" (John 17:21–23). In this chapter, my aim is to dig deeper into what

---

1. These are references to the shows' theme songs. Look it up.

happens when we stop thinking about the faith as an exchange of verdicts and start seeing it as an exchange of persons, living as though love, and not law, were the thing that really mattered.

Adventures in Babysitting

For the last several months, my kids have been obsessed with all things *Star Wars* (of which I'm quite proud). As I have revisited George Lucas's universe with my children, I have noticed that a common thread in the original three films (I refuse to even acknowledge the existence of the prequels other than for purposes of mockery and dismissal) is that of awakening. The more Luke Skywalker learns about the universe outside his home planet of Tatooine, the more he feels he can no longer continue to waste his days as a moisture farmer on his remote desert home. As his mentor Obi-Wan says to him after initiating him into the ways of the Force, "You've just taken your first step into a larger world." (In fact, even Luke's companion Han Solo's initial scoffing and skepticism—"Hokie religions and ancient weapons are no match for a good blaster at your side"—gradually subside as he finds himself a participant in a narrative and movement larger than himself and satisfying his own greed. And by the time the events of episode seven roll around, he's a complete believer.) For our hero, Luke, the confines of his native world and the guardianship of his uncle and aunt become too constricting once his eyes are opened to the "larger world" for which he is destined.

Something quite similar can be said of the people of God. In Galatians we read:

> Now before faith came, we were held captive under the law, imprisoned until the coming faith would be revealed. So then, the law was our guardian until Christ came, in order that we might be justified by faith. But now that faith has come, we are no longer under a guardian, for in Christ Jesus you are all sons of God, through faith. For as many of you as were baptized into Christ have put on Christ. There is neither Jew nor Greek, there is neither slave nor free, there is no male and female, for you are all one in Christ Jesus. And if you are Christ's, then you are Abraham's offspring, heirs according to promise.
>
> I mean that the heir, as long as he is a child, is no different from a slave, though he is the owner of everything, but he is under guardians and managers until the date set by his father. In the same way we also, when we were children, were enslaved to the elementary principles of the world. But when the fullness of time had come, God sent forth his Son, born of woman, born under the law, to redeem those who were under the law, so that we might receive adoption as sons. And because you are sons, God has sent the Spirit of his Son into our hearts, crying, "Abba! Fa-

ther!" So you are no longer a slave, but a son, and if a son, then an heir through God. (Gal. 3:23–4:7)

While much more could be said about this passage of Scripture, I would like to highlight something that began to dawn on me during my years in seminary, the significance of which eventually played a huge role in leading me into the Catholic Church. What the apostle is describing in these verses is the historical progression of God's people from the confines of the Old Covenant to the liberty of the New. In other words, when God's people were "under the law [of Moses]," their experience was one of slavery and bondage. In fact, the word that is translated as "guardian" in the passage above (as in "the law was our *guardian* until Christ came. . . . But now that faith has come, we are no longer under a *guardian*") is the Greek word from which we get our English word *pedagogue,* and its original meaning denoted something like "babysitter" (not so much the dispensable paid-by-the-hour kind but more like the live-in Mary Poppins kind). Israelites under the law, then, were truly God's people, but they were like minors, little children who are heirs to a massive inheritance that they won't be able to enjoy until they reach the age of maturity. In that regard, Paul says, their experience differs little from that of the household slaves. Like Luke Skywalker, the people of God under the old system knew they were destined for something greater than the guardianship and bondage they presently experienced, but they still had to await the appointed time to enter into it.

"In the fullness of time," the apostle writes, "God sent forth his Son . . . to redeem those who were under the law, so that we might receive adoption as sons." The coming of Christ signaled the passage of the people of God from our minority to our majority, from our juvenile and slavish status to our current status as full-grown sons and heirs of all our heavenly Father possesses.[2] The monumental and cataclysmic nature of this shift from the Old to the New cannot be overstated. As I was digging into the implications of these things as a seminary student (implications I'm still discovering to this day), I would often meet resistance from some professors and fellow students when I tried to articulate the conclusions I had been reaching. "If we are no longer 'under the law,'" I would insist, "then that means we no longer have to approach God as fearful subjects or trembling supplicants, but we can boldly approach him as sons whom he loves more than any earthly parent could ever love his or her own children. As Paul says in Galatians 4, God has replaced the demands of the law with the gift of the Spirit who brings our sonship to bear upon our lives and makes loving him a present reality." While I got some nodding heads and agreement here and there, I also got plenty of sideways looks and

---

2. In antiquity it was the sons in particular who received the father's inheritance, which is why the apostle appeals to male imagery here (and not because he is sexist). But if it makes my female readers feel any better about being referred to as "sons," the New Testament elsewhere refers to us all as "the Bride of Christ"!

askance glances. Law still took precedent over love, if not explicitly then at least implicitly, and to state that the coming of Christ introduced a way of life that was so unlike the old one that fear and guilt were now foreign concepts was taking this whole "family" dynamic idea too far.

Beginning to Love

One of my favorite films is *The Matrix,* which introduces us to Thomas Anderson, aka "Neo," a man who is naggingly disaffected with his experience of the world. He knows there are answers to his questions, the main one of which (though he can't account for why he's asking it) is "What is the Matrix?" Through a series of pretty mind-blowing events, he is introduced to Morpheus, the man who can answer his questions and explain his lingering dissatisfaction with life as he knows it. What Neo learns is that the world as we all experience it is an illusion, a massive virtual reality program known as the Matrix, whose job is to lull us to sleep by keeping us in our pointless lives and meaningless jobs, longing for the things we believe will make us happy (but ultimately won't). So if this physical world is an illusion, where are we, really? This is where it gets even weirder. Every person we see every day is just a digital avatar—and we all really exist plugged in to coffinlike pods where we function like batteries to keep the machine working. Morpheus's role is to set people free from the Matrix, unplug them from their cocoons, and gather them together as a resistance movement against the entire system.

Here's where it gets tricky. These freedom fighters, led by Morpheus, can reinsert themselves into the Matrix and thereby reenter this world, but when they do, they are hunted by deadly agents whose aim is to exterminate them and quash the resistance. The question arises, "If you die while in the Matrix, do you die in real life?" The answer given is that our minds are so trained to believe that the Matrix's virtual reality is in fact real, that yes, being killed in the Matrix results in death in the real world. What eventually demonstrates Neo's uniqueness, however, is that he alone gradually gains the ability to truly believe that the so-called material world that our five senses seem to mediate really is just an illusion (or, to borrow from one of the film's best scenes, the secret to bending a spoon with your mind is realizing that "there is no spoon").

This "awakening" (to piggyback on my *Star Wars* analogy) is fully manifested in the film's climactic scene where the deadly Agent Smith pursues Neo. Instead of fleeing for his life as his fellow resistance fighters do, Neo stops, faces his opponent, and begins to fight against him exhibiting the ability to alter "reality," act with superhuman speed, and break the laws that bind the rest of us (even to the point of stopping a bullet in midair, snatching it between his thumb and forefinger, and dropping it to the ground). By this point, when Neo looks around the Matrix, he doesn't see what we all see. He sees the computer code behind it. He knows that he is no longer subject to the rulebook that shackles the rest of us. When one of the rebels asks how Neo can display such fearlessness, Morpheus responds, "He is beginning to believe."

As my own eyes were slowly adjusting to the Catholic gospel and the misfit faith that accompanied it, it occurred to me that a similar shift was in store, one no less apocalyptic than Neo's:

> By this we know that we abide in him and he in us, because he has given us of his Spirit. . . . So we have come to know and to believe the love that God has for us. God is love, and whoever abides in love abides in God, and God abides in him. By this is love perfected with us, so that we may have confidence for the day of judgment, because as he is so also are we in this world. There is no fear in love, but perfect love casts out fear. For fear has to do with punishment, and whoever fears has not been perfected in love. We love because he first loved us. (1 John 4:13, 16–19)

Here John picks up right where we left Paul in Galatians, with the gift of the Holy Spirit that is so central to the New Covenant. He goes on to explain that it is the Spirit that brings about the cataclysmic shift from law to love that Jesus inaugurated in his death and resurrection. John is saying here what I was desperately trying to grasp back in my seminary days (and even farther back, during my days at Calvary

Chapel both in the United States and in Europe): Love has conquered Law, and the divine economy is no longer characterized by the themes of slavery, bondage, guilt, and fear as it was in times past under the Old Covenant. To use John's words, "There is no fear in love, but perfect love casts out fear," and therefore "we may have confidence for the day of judgment." He puts it this way a chapter earlier: "Whenever our heart condemns us, God is greater than our heart" (1 John 3:20).

Once Neo began to believe the truth about the Matrix, he was no longer subject to its rulebook or laws but could disregard them completely. Similarly, once we become convinced that the Spirit bears his fruit of love in our hearts, we no longer need to subject ourselves to the tenets of the old system or live according to the way things used to be. As the New Testament makes absolutely clear, love fulfills the law, and if "God is love" and pours forth his love in our hearts by his Spirit (Rom. 5:5), then there is absolutely no need to give any ground to guilt, fear of hell, or any such thing.

Now, I realize that some of you may be thinking, *No shit, Sherlock! This isn't exactly news to us. We've known it the whole time.* Well, maybe that's true (and surely a reminder couldn't hurt?), but if your story is at all like mine, this transition I'm describing has been anything but ordinary and the conclusion anything but foregone. You see, according to my former mind-set, God didn't *do away with* the system of law so much as radically *capitulate to* it. The point of the cross, according to my old way of thinking, was not to *obliterate* the former legal arrangement of debts and payments but rather to eternally *validate* it: We owed God a debt, and the punishment for not paying it is torment in hell. Jesus (this view says) ponied up that payment by suffering a punishment at the hands of God tantamount to eternal torment in hell so that God could then be free to offer his chosen ones that forensic pardon that we believed was so central to the gospel. Do you see the point I'm making here? The legal understanding of the gospel that I once embraced not only fails to usher in anything new but actually doubles down on the old! It says, in essence, "Yes, it really is all about law." For in this paradigm, law, and not love, gets the last word.

A Better Word

But the last word, I came to realize, needs to go to grace and to mercy. There simply is no other way to couch this love story about a divine Father and his quest for a worldwide and universal family with whom to share his very essence, nature, and self. Any system that strikes fear into the hearts of God's children, is law and not gospel.

> For you have not come to [Mount Sinai, that] may be touched, a blazing fire and darkness and gloom and a tempest and the sound of a trumpet and a voice

whose words made the hearers beg that no further messages be spoken to them. For they could not endure the order that was given, "If even a beast touches the mountain, it shall be stoned." Indeed, so terrifying was the sight that Moses said, "I tremble with fear."

But you have come to Mount Zion and to the city of the living God, the heavenly Jerusalem, and to innumerable angels in festal gathering, and to the assembly of the firstborn who are enrolled in heaven, and to God, the judge of all, and to the spirits of the righteous made perfect, and to Jesus, the mediator of a new covenant, and to *the sprinkled blood that speaks a better word than the blood of Abel.* (Heb. 12:18–24, emphasis added)

The "blood of Abel" cried for vengeance, which the Mosaic Law threatened for any who transgressed its commands. (I have always dug the old King James rendering of Moses's response to receiving the Law on Mount Sinai: "I exceedingly fear and quake.") But the blood of Christ, Hebrews says, "speaks a better word," one that assures us that the entire old way has been abolished, that the system of the law has been destroyed, and that guilt and sin have been removed from us "as far as the east is from the west" (Ps. 103:12).

I'm going to draw a connection here that, as a grown man, I'm slightly ashamed to make. But before I do, I would like to submit (for the record) that I play sports, like to drink beer, have completed three full rounds of P90X, and once beat a guy at arm wrestling even though he was way bigger than me. With that said, *Annie* is pretty awesome. Yes, I'm talking about the story about the little orphan girl from the 1940s who would stay up every night gazing out the orphanage window and singing songs about whether her real parents are young, smart, and collect things like ashtrays and art. (I know all the words. So what? I'd totally kick your ass at arm wrestling, just so you know.) The scene that sticks out for me at the moment is when Annie, much to her shock and surprise, is chosen to stay for a period of time with the wealthy philanthropist Oliver Warbucks. Upon arriving and surveying his palatial mansion, she is asked, "What would you like to do first?" Her response: "First the windows, then the floors." Now, we as the audience chuckle at this little misunderstanding on Annie's part. "*Adorable*," we say. But the moment is indeed profound. Annie is so stuck in her slavish mentality that she doesn't know how to self-identify as anything other than some laborer for hire. All she has ever known is her menial (and seemingly meaningless) existence in that orphanage, and she simply doesn't have the ability to disembed herself from her former reality and acclimate to her new station as an eventual adoptee and heiress of a massive fortune. 'Stead've treated, she gets tricked; 'stead've kisses, she gets kicked. Hashtag, It'saHardKnockLife (and it always had been).

I have come to discover on my own spiritual journey that, in a myriad of ways, I am stuck in that old servile mentality, according to which guilt, shame, fear, and condemnation are all considered legitimate things to feel as a child of God. But a faith that is slavish, and a relationship with God that makes me feel like some expendable, hired-on orphan isn't enough for me. It's not enough for you, either. And you *know* it.

Guilt vs. Grown-Up Spirituality

Let's take a moment and talk about *guilt* (not in a morbid way but hopefully in a constructive and encouraging one!). When we hear that word, we usually think of a trial where a judge weighs the good things we've done against the bad so that he can render a verdict about our standing before the law. Now, I don't want to discount this idea completely, but come on, let's be honest: We don't apply the term *guilt* to our own children, do we? I know I don't—as in, I literally *never* look at my nine-year-old son Maddoc and, with a heart filled with love, *proclaim him not guilty*. The idea would be comical if it weren't so ridiculous. He's my boy, for crying out loud! As his dad, I just love him, no matter what.

Likewise, the more we are stuck in a mind-set that tells us that the good news is that God sees us as "not guilty," we are little better off than Annie when she got all excited to wash the windows of a nicer building than those she usually washed: Sure, she is still a slave-orphan, but at least this is a change of scenery. (And the sponges are nicer here and everything!) It's the same with us and God. We miss the whole point of the gospel if our attitude is "Yay! God doesn't even hate me all that much! Maybe I'll even get picked for plunger duty in heaven's men's room—if I don't get cast headlong into the flames of eternal torment for irritating him, that is!" We need to start relating to God as a Father, is what I'm saying.

"Where, then," you may be wondering, "does *sin* fit into all this?" It's a fair question. If God is before anything else our Father, and if earthly fathers scoff at the idea of beholding their own children through the lens of law and its corresponding notions of sin and guilt, are these concepts foreign to God as well? Obviously not. While the New Testament doesn't emphasize sin in the same way that the Old does, the idea is not altogether absent. Perhaps most famously, the apostle John writes: "If we confess our sins, [God] is faithful and just to forgive us our sins and to cleanse us from all unrighteousness" (1 John 1:9). Is there a way to understand passages like this without falling back into a mind-set that is servile, slavish, and merely legal? Is it possible to enjoy a familial relationship with a God who sometimes dons a black robe and gavel?

Of course it is. If there is one thing I've learned over the past few years, it's that Obi-Wan Kenobi was onto something when he said, "Luke, you're going to find that many of the truths we cling to depend greatly on our own point of view." (Hey, I told you my kids have got me on a *Star Wars* kick—deal with it. Otherwise I'd be quoting U2 lyrics on every page.) What I mean is that Scripture presents us with a multifaceted God, a God who allows himself to be described in myriad metaphors. I have argued enough already that divine fatherhood is primary since it's what God is by nature, so I will add here only that it's easy to allow other biblical metaphors to usurp an undue and disproportionate place in our relationship with him. If we fixate upon those depictions of God that emphasize his judgeship or anger, for example (and there are some), we can wind up with an unbalanced understanding of who he is and who we are before him. But when we step back and see the entire biblical story, we clearly see a loving Father who at times must judge or punish (what loving father doesn't?), but even in those acts that are more stern and official, his fatherhood always shines through.

How does this relate to the issue of sin and guilt? It relates in a massive and even transformative way! I have come to realize that when I "sin" (which I do daily, hourly even), I can think of it in a couple of different ways. One way is to say, "I have broken God's holy law and have thereby rendered myself a potential victim of his strict and unbending justice. Until I gain acquittal I am in danger of the eternal punishment to which my lawlessness has subjected me." *Barf.* Now, I don't mean to sound dismissive or overly cavalier here, but speaking very personally, I have little room for a relationship with God that smacks of this kind of remote, formal, and forensic dynamic. Not anymore, anyway. The more I fall prey to this skewed mentality, the more skewed my relationship with God will likely become. The less room I give to God's fatherhood, the less I will feel like his child in my own personal experience.

But there's another way I can respond to my own sin, one that is more consistent with the view of God I have come to discover and embrace. When I sin, I reveal my own humanity and brokenness—I put on full display for all to see the fact that I'm weak and full of failure. While I may look at the ideal with approval and admiration, I often fall far short of meeting it. When this happens, how do I imagine God responds? Does he seethe with wrath and diabolically twist his mustache and lick his retributive chops, eagerly anticipating the moment when he will Chinese-water-torture me for a trillion years? Because that doesn't sound very paternal or loving to me! "But hang on," you may be thinking. "You're not being exactly fair here. God is obviously not some cosmic sadist, but he is still bound by his nature, which is holy and must punish sin. He may take no pleasure in it, but he has no choice but to disinherit those who sin against him. The purity of his very character demands it." The idea here is that God cannot but see our sin as creating a chasm between himself and us, perhaps even an eternally separating one.

I have several potential words I could use in response to this, but I'll opt for something refined and British: *bollocks*. The idea that the all-powerful, sovereign king of the universe is somehow *bound* by something is patently ridiculous. And further, consider what he is supposedly bound by! What this view is saying is that God, despite the fatherly love that he has for his children and the divine power at his fingertips to save us, can by my sin find himself so stuck, so backed into a corner, so hamstrung by schizophrenia that he is left with *no other choice* but to hurl me headlong into a yawning fiery chasm of brimstone and sulfur, where he will keep me conscious enough to actually feel the anguish of his vindictive rage for sideways-eight years. I'm sorry, but a "God" like this may instill fear, but he won't inspire love. Forget love—it'd be hard enough to even like him. I mean, he sounds like kind of a prick if you want to know the truth.

Rather than assuming that every time we sin, God is forced against his will to respond in ways utterly uncharacteristic of true fatherhood, why not treat him like the loving Father we know he is? Just last night my seven-year-old daughter was crying at the kitchen table because she thought (incorrectly) that I was upset over something she did. ("I wish I could be good for once!" were her words. She's very dramatic.) Obviously, my heart broke. I explained to her that I loved her, that she didn't do anything wrong, and even if she did, it wouldn't change how I feel about her. I said these things because I'm her dad, and because any effort on her part to be "good" and any remorse over being "bad" is adorable. Is it that much of a stretch to think that God looks at his own children that way? That far from being forced at gunpoint to hate us, he actually loves us when we succeed as well as when we blow it? When we fall short of God's ideal, therefore, we ought to respond the way we want our kids to respond to us when they've been bad. If my children cower in fear before me, that says something about my parenting skills (read: *they suck*). Likewise, if we cower in fear before God when we sin, it suggests an implicit fear of his anger and retribution toward us. But when we see him as a Father and not as a judge, our failures will only provide him opportunities to be fatherly (which, as I've been arguing, is sort of his thing).

Let me take this a step further. The mentality of my daughter—her desire to be "good" rather than "bad"—is obviously quite juvenile (which makes perfect sense given her age). All kids are like that. For example, one of my kids will ask, "Dad, is [such-and-such, a character in a movie] a good guy or a bad guy?" These are way harder questions to answer than they initially appear! Is Jabba the Hutt a "bad guy"? Well, from a child's perspective, he certainly is: He's creepy and disgusting, he has Han Solo encased in carbonite as a decoration in his main hall, and he attempts to kill Luke Skywalker not once but twice. Textbook "bad guy," right? But not so fast. The whole reason Jabba has been after Han Solo is that Han owes him a bunch of money and has refused to pay it back. (And Han, don't forget, is a smuggler, a trafficker of illegal contraband: drugs, weapons, sex slaves, who knows? The guy doesn't exactly have a functioning moral compass.) From Jabba's vantage point, he is just being a good businessman (or slug, or whatever the hell he is), protecting his investment and taking steps to avoid defaults on future loans. The same is true of Darth Vader. In fact, I attempted to explain to my children the other day how unlikely it would be that the "bad guys" in *Star Wars* would actually refer to it as "the *dark side* of the Force," since no one really thinks they're actually on the side of darkness and evil. (I'm not sure my postmodern argument for multiperspectivalism really landed though.) But whatever. Such a black-and-white interpretation of reality is sort of unsophisticated, is what I'm getting at.

And God agrees. We have already seen that Paul likened the era during which Israel was under the jurisdiction of the law to a child under the watchful eye of a babysitter. But to further flesh this all out, I want to call into question an assumption that many people make. The way we often think about the relationship of sin to the law goes something like this: "Sins are the bad things we do, and the law comes in to point out that those things are bad and to tell us to quit doing them." Pretty basic, right? The problem is that this is completely wrong! Consider these statements from Paul:

> Now *the law came in to increase the trespass,* but where sin increased, grace abounded all the more. (Rom. 5:20, emphasis added)

> Likewise, my brothers, you also have died to the law through the body of Christ. . . . For while we were living in the flesh, *our sinful passions, aroused by the law,*

were at work in our members to bear fruit for death. But now we are released from the law, having died to that which held us captive, so that we serve in the new way of the Spirit and not in the old way of the written code. . . . But *sin, seizing an opportunity through the commandment,* produced in me all kinds of covetousness. For *apart from the law, sin lies dead.* I was once alive apart from the law, but *when the commandment came, sin came alive* and I died. *The very commandment* that promised life *proved to be death to me.* For *sin, seizing an opportunity through the commandment,* deceived me and through it killed me. . . . It was *sin, producing death in me through what is good,* in order that sin might be shown to be *sin,* and *through the commandment might become sinful beyond measure.* (Rom. 7:4a, 5–6, 8–11, 13b, emphasis added)

What the apostle says is pretty mind-blowing. Was the law's job simply to follow sin around and point its accusatory finger? No. "The law came in to increase the [sin]," says Paul. It was the law that "aroused our sinful passions" and allowed sin to "seize an opportunity," even to the point where the law "revived sin." Thus the law "proved to be death" and actually "produced death," thereby making sin "sinful beyond measure." In fact, the connection between the law and sin was so intimate under the Old Covenant that Paul actually had to dispel the idea that the two were the same thing, that the law was itself sin (Rom. 7:7).

Now, let's pause, step back, and consider the ramifications of all this. As I have said, my kids' preoccupation with "good guys" versus "bad guys" is juvenile, and likewise, Israel's days under the watchful eye of Moses's law were the same: they were being babysat until they grew up and could handle adult levels of responsibility. What does this have to do with us today? As long as we understand our relationship with God in terms of lists of do's and don'ts, we will be stuck in a place of childish suspended animation, frozen in prepubescence, when God wants us free from such shackles and impediments to mature to full-grown spirituality.

The apostle Paul challenged the Colossian believers along these same lines, asking them why, if they had been united to the risen Christ, they were allowing others to judge them about nitpicky religious matters that "are a shadow of things to come, but the substance belongs to Christ" (2:16–17). "Why," he continues, "do you submit to regulations—'Do not handle, do not taste, do not touch'?" (2:20–21). Relating to God on this basis—as though it were obedience to outward commands that ultimately mattered—is to stop far short of genuine spirituality. It's not about jumping through hoops but about loving God by loving our neighbor. As Paul explained to the Corinthians, "'All things are lawful,' but not all things are helpful. 'All things are lawful,' but not all things build up. Let no one seek his own good, but the good of his neighbor" (1 Cor. 10:23–24).

Grow up, is my point. If you want to remain in a state of stunted growth and law-driven, guilt-grounded, fearful

Christianity, knock yourself out. Be like Annie and scrub those windows, hoping that your strict Miss Hannigan of a God won't wake up angry and drop you into that lake of fire. But if, like me, you have come to wonder whether that kind of Christianity is really sustainable over the long haul, then perhaps it's time to push "further up and further in" to a deeper, fuller, and more mature form of faith. Rather than seeing the great command ("You shall love the Lord your God with all your heart, mind, and strength") as Law 2.0, we should recalibrate our attitude and begin to realize that "God is Love," and rather than demanding he be the object of our love upon threat of hell for the smallest withholding, accept that he is present and pleased whenever we sincerely love in deed and truth, with our hearts as well as our hands.

"When I was a child," wrote Paul, "I spoke as a child, I understood as a child, I thought as a child; but when I became a man, I put away childish things." As long as you think you've got it all figured out (with proper beliefs and stellar morals), you will have a hard time appreciating much of what I've been saying. To quote Bono, "You never knew love, until you crossed the line of grace." When we not only recognize ourselves as misfit screwups but embrace that identity, we will finally begin to see God as a Father and to see love, rather than law, as the point of everything. "And now abide faith, hope, love, these three; but the greatest of these is love" (1 Cor. 13:11, 13, NKJV).

—————————————————————————————

4

Unity in Diversity

(Or, We're One But We're
Not the Same)

—————————————————————————————

Forests, Trees, and Baseball

"Enthusiasms," muses Al Capone (masterfully played by Robert De Niro) in the 1987 film *The Untouchables*. "What are mine? What draws my admiration? What is that which gives me joy?" In this early scene, Capone is at a formal dinner with his trusted underlings, one of whom has betrayed him. As he circles the table making his twisted motivational speech, his goons seek to correctly answer his question with things like "Dames!" and "Boozin'!" Capone smirks and shakes his head. "Baseball!" he says, at which the room fills with obsequious, mandatory laughter. He then brandishes a bat and reminds them that, while hitting is an individual effort, all the base hits in the world don't matter if the men are not team players when out in the field. At this point Capone is standing directly behind his betrayer, but unlike in a similar scene in an upper room a couple thousand years ago involving a betrayer and the Betrayed, there is no gesture of peace or last-ditch offer of friendship and pardon. Instead, well, you can probably imagine what happens next: Capone caves the guy's skull in with the baseball bat, the blood slowly oozes across the lavish table, and everyone learns a valuable lesson about teamwork and solidarity (shudder).

The issue of individual effort versus teamwork, and the paradox of true unity and real diversity, is highlighted not only in the realm of baseball but also, you guessed it, in the mystery of the Trinity. There we behold something ineffable and beyond comprehension: There is one God, but that one God subsists in three coequal and coeternal divine Persons—the Father, the Son, and the Holy Spirit. The Father is not the Son or the Spirit, but he is God. The Son is also God, although he is not the Spirit or the Father. And the Spirit is God, yet he is not the Father or the Son. And all the while there are not three Gods but one. The baffling and counterintuitive nature of this mystery has been captured in a funny way (to me at least) by a meme that I saw going around Facebook in which Jesus is kneeling in prayer and looking up to heaven. The caption reads, "Are you there, God? It's me, you." (Now, I understand that this meme was probably created by those whose intent was to mock the idea of the Trinity, that God can be three-in-one. But let's lighten up and be honest for a moment: The whole thing is a bit ridiculous, isn't it? From the perspective of conventional wisdom anyway. Isn't that why we refer to it as a "mystery"?)

But when we set aside our desire to understand the Triune nature of the one God and simply accept the whole thing as an article of faith, we can finally see that actual unity and actual diversity can exist together. What I hope to show in this chapter is that, just as there is diversity in the one God, so there is diversity all around us in this world. So if we claim to love this diverse God, we had better love our diverse neighbors as well. Even when they're weird.

Fear of the Other

We humans seem to be rather sectarian (or at least it's our knee-jerk response to being confronted with things we consider strange, foreign, or odd). Perhaps a better label than *sectarian* is *xenophobic,* which comes from the Greek words *xenos* (stranger) and *phobos* (fear). Xenophobia is the fear of the stranger, a deep mistrust of the unfamiliar "other." An embodiment of this psychosis can be found in Ron Swanson, a character from NBC's *Parks and Recreation.* A staunch libertarian and hater of the government (despite working for the city of Pawnee, Indiana, in the Parks Department), Ron is the epitome of intolerance and suspicion of anything he finds exotic and untraditional. Some of his well-known mottoes and principles include:

> "There's only one thing I hate more than lying—skim milk, which is water that is lying about being milk."

"Fish, for sport only, not for meat. Fish meat is practically a vegetable."

Ron is not completely closed-minded, of course. Although he "doesn't care for ethnic food," he was once persuaded to try a burrito. ("You had me at 'meat tornado.'") Another time he branched out even further: "There is a hot spinning cone of meat in that Greek restaurant next door. I don't know what it is, but I'd like to eat the whole thing." A couple of other television shows provide even clearer examples of xenophobia: ABC's *Lost* and HBO's *Game of Thrones*, both of which actually have groups of people whom the protagonists refer to as "the Others" (although to be fair, the fear of strangers in these cases is pretty justified).

My point is that fear of the strange and unfamiliar is exceedingly common. In fact, often what is labeled as "racist" is really xenophobia—we encounter practices with which we're unfamiliar or hear languages spoken that we can't understand, and we react in fear (or anger because, well, we're fearful). A perfect example is the way many evangelical Christians initially responded to Mitt Romney's candidacy for president in 2012: "He's a *Mormon!*" we heard. "Do we really want one of *those people* as president? I mean, look at what they believe! Humans will someday become gods? It's preposterous!" The irony here is so thick you can cut it with the knife that we believe God told Abraham to stab his own kid with. See my point? Traditional Christianity teaches some pretty wacky things too. For example, we are taught to believe that God wiped out the entire human race in a worldwide flood, saving only Noah, his family, and all the animals in a huge boat that Noah built out of gopher wood. There's also a part in our Bible where God made the sun stand still in the sky long enough for Joshua to finish killing a bunch of guys. That's kind of weird. Let's see, what else? Oh, right: *the resurrection of Christ from the dead.* Talk about a counterintuitive, outside-the-box thing to believe in! And yet because it's so familiar and culturally ingrained, it doesn't strike us as in the least bit odd. Mormons, though? Those guys are nuts.

Perhaps the clearest biblical teaching about our treatment of the "other" comes from the lips of Jesus himself, unsurprisingly. In Luke 10:25–37 Jesus tells a story about a man who was traveling from one city to another and was attacked by thieves who robbed him, beat him senseless, and left him by the side of the road to die. (Just think of it as the fate of pretty much anyone who ventured outside after dark in New York City in the 1970s.) A priest came along, and later a Levite, but they both crossed the road to avoid the man. But then a Samaritan happened upon the scene, and despite the hatred that existed between Samaritans and Jews, he dressed the victim's wounds, put him on his horse, and took him to a nearby inn where he paid in advance for the man's stay until he was well enough to leave. What makes this story remarkable is the exchange that initially occasioned it. A lawyer had asked Jesus what was necessary for gaining eternal life, and Jesus (as was his custom) answered his question with one of his own: "What do you think the law says about this?" The man responded, "Love God and love my neighbor," to which Jesus replied, "Bingo." But the matter was far from settled. "And who exactly counts as my neighbor?" the man pressed. Jesus then gave the parable of "the good Samaritan" and afterward asked, "Which of these three was 'neighbor' to the dying man?" (The question defined the issue as determining not simply who our neighbor is but whether we are good ones ourselves.) The crowd had no choice but to admit that it was the despised Samaritan—the "other" if there ever was one—who had fulfilled the law through his mercy and compassion. The Jewish lawyer's question ("What must I do to inherit eternal life?") was answered by Jesus in an ironic and counterintuitive way that challenged his kinsmen's xenophobia ("Be like this Samaritan").

While I personally was never much of a cultural xenophobe, I did dabble. When I first moved to Africa at eighteen, for example, I obviously experienced a bit of culture shock. I remember being put off the first time I made plans to meet a friend from my village at noon and he strolled up at two p.m. To my question about why he was so late, I received the response, "This is Africa!" *Allll*-righty then, how silly of me to expect promptness! In this person's defense, I soon learned he probably had to stop by the post office and mail a letter on his way to meet me, which in Africa can require all of Wednesday to accomplish. But once I grew accustomed to how long it takes to do the simplest tasks, I understood a bit more the mind-set of "soft time" they adopted there.

Similarly, when I moved to Europe when I was twenty-one, I exhibited some intolerance toward the aspects of that culture that were strange to me as a native Californian. For instance, when you enter a market in Budapest, you must grab a handheld shopping basket. You *must*. It is not an option—it's law. In fact, perched by the entrance will most likely be a two-hundred-year-old woman, wearing some white smocklike garment, whose sole purpose in life is to make sure you take one. Oh, you're not planning to actually buy anything? *Irrelevant! Grab a #@$% basket or get the hell out.* I eventually came to see the humor in situations like that, but initially it really irritated me that someone would create a little basket fiefdom and then guard it as if their entire life depended on it.

As long as I thought I had all the answers (whether culturally or theologically), I could easily relegate everyone else to some category of inferiority—they were either too liberal or too conservative, too Pentecostal or too Baptist, too contemporary or too traditional, too successful to be uncompromised or too deliberately irrelevant to be taken seriously. But becoming a crashed-and-burned misfit—in addition to totally sucking—really helped with the whole "judge not" thing.

Reaching Across the Aisle

Funny thing about paradigm shifts: Once everything you previously believed starts to crumble around you, and the idols you were so certain of become dashed to pieces at your feet, the effect can be a bit humbling. In fact, the more sure a person is of himself, the more profound will be the resulting level of embarrassment when he has to issue a mea culpa and then spend the next few years eating crow. That certainly has been the case with me, to the point where (as I mentioned in the Introduction), after submitting the final manuscript of this book, I asked my editor if I could scrap the entire thing and start over from scratch. The original version was too polemical and smacked of too much certainty, and if I have learned anything from my transition out of Protestant ministry into a more open-minded Catholicism (and I hope I have learned lots of things), it's that I need to temper my zeal with prudence and remember that I have been wrong before about things that I was absolutely sure were right.

Until a person gains a certain level of expertise on a given subject, he is unlikely to recognize how little he knows about everything else. (Correspondingly, the more trained he is in one subject, the quicker he will be to know his limitations concerning all the other ones.) And to piggyback on that, if he comes to a place where he needs to recant much of what he once thought about the subject on which he was supposedly an expert, then the only respectable way forward must involve a whole hell of a lot of humility. For instance, if someone earns a doctorate in political science, the sheer amount of effort, toil, and tears it took to gain that level of knowledge would cause the person to realize that other subjects have their own experts too. So when the Ph.D. in political science is discussing environmental issues with a friend, he should be the first to realize his own limitations on this other matter. And further, if in midcareer he recants his American-style libertarianism and espouses democratic socialism, he'd better dial down the hubris when he does it, as well as remind himself to hold *all* his positions with a little lighter grip from now on.

This is precisely the position I find myself in (although my theology degree is only a master's and not a doctorate). Actually becoming one of the "others" whom I once villainized by quitting my ministry and associating with the very group that my old denomination officially labeled "the Antichrist" has forced me to rein in my zeal, to temper my excitement and certainty about the new things I have been discovering over the last several years. In fact, many of my efforts of late have been centered on extricating myself from the religious spotlight—I shut down my old blog, I took myself off the speaking circuit roster, I tried to back out of this book project—and creating space to give expression to certain thoughts and ideas that I know will leave a bad taste in religious people's mouths. (My podcast is called *Drunk Ex-Pastors,* for crying out loud.) Something just doesn't feel right about the triumphalistic chest-thumping proclamation that I've discovered "the truth" when that truth is in many ways the opposite of the one I was trumpeting beforehand. It just seems uncouth. Untoward, even. I like obsolete words.

My point in all this is that my own paradigm shift, my own experience of losing my footing and having the ground beneath me give way, has left me feeling vulnerable and shaky. But that shakiness and vulnerability have produced at least one good by-product that I can think of: they have made me more open to the tentative and incomplete nature of my current positions as well as to the validity of the views of others that I find unfamiliar and perhaps a bit weird. The refrain I have found myself repeating over and over again lately is "There's something to everything," regardless of how foreign or taboo the issue or opinion may be. Coming face to face with the provisional nature of my own theological views (and doing so very publicly) has caused me to be loath to dismiss the views of others—whether theological or otherwise—since, after all, by keeping my mouth shut and ears and heart open, I just might learn something.

There's a certain irony here, a "black fly in your Chardonnay," if you will.[1] As many of my Protestant friends have pointed out (with no small amount of glee), becoming Catholic only to embrace my inner agnostic is precisely

---

1. Has anyone else noticed that the fact that none of the examples of irony in Alanis Morrisette's song "Ironic" is actual irony is *itself* what makes the song "Ironic" ironic? I know, blew your mind, right? Begin slow-clap now . . .

bass-ackwards, since the whole point of Catholicism is supposedly its ability to give its devotees the kind of certitude about its dogmas that Protestantism cannot deliver: "Geez, if you wanted to become a wishy-washy epistemological hippie, you should've stayed on our team! But joining the Certainty Society only to embrace doubt is as bizarre as joining the Tea Party in order to explore multiculturalism." And there's a sense in which they're absolutely right. I'm kind of a shitty Catholic. And all I can muster by way of response is that it's not the first time I've missed the point entirely, and we've already established that it's okay to suck at something worthwhile.

Arriving at a place where we can reach across the aisle and find beauty and humanity in the views of the other is never easy. If you honestly hope to find true unity in diversity, I caution you to be careful what you wish for. While it is very freeing to not be constantly threatened by the unfamiliar, the humiliation that such freedom requires beforehand really blows.

Searching for Common Ground

I have found that in order to celebrate that "true Trinitarian unity in diversity" I mentioned above, you must first be open and willing to look for it. This may require the kind of humbling paradigm shift I have been describing in my own life, or it may not. But either way, a celebration of our commonality with the other must be preceded by a sincere desire to find it, even when that discovery is difficult and painstaking. For example, when you're confronted with the Jehovah's Witness at your door or the atheist in your philosophy classroom, common ground may not be initially easy to find. After all, the guy in the first example is a "brainwashed cult member" while the second person "hates Jesus." What's the point of even trying with these people?

But this kind of first impression gets things off on the wrong foot, and it takes a healthy dose of humility and charity for us to realize this and overcome it. Let's take the case of the J-Dub mentioned above: Does he think he is brainwashed? Does he consider himself in a cult? Of course not, and in fact, he may very well think those things about you! So rather than employ the "I know you are but what am I?" approach, someone needs to be the bigger person and seek to bridge the gap that separates you. (And obviously I think I should be the one to do it if it's me in this situation, as should you if you are.) In the case of our proverbial "cultist," the first thing we need to do is recognize that he is incredibly dedicated to his faith. (Otherwise why would anyone commit social suicide by being a door-to-door Jesus salesman?) His desire to please God (in his case, "Jehovah") is clearly paramount, which can be a huge touchstone and an opportunity to find common ground. Now, if he sticks to his script, which such people are trained to do, he will seek to show you why you are wrong and he is right. In my experience, I have found that there is little profit in engaging on that level. He will trot out his proof-texts, and you will adduce yours, and what will inevitably ensue will be little better than a playground-style "Nuh-uh"/"Yeah-huh" stand-off with no winners, only losers. But if we take the approach of simply refusing to debate our religious differences (significant though they are) and instead seek to love this person since he's not a *cultist* but our *neighbor,* then we may not win the debate, but so what? While failing to "convert the enemy to our side" (which, let's be honest, wasn't going to happen anyway), we will have nonetheless succeeded in actually seeing him as something beyond a nuisance, an other, or a joke. And who knows? Maybe at some dark or difficult moment in this man's life, he will remember being seen and loved by us and regarded as a sharer and coparticipant in this mysterious thing we call human nature. And even if we made no impression on him whatsoever, at least we got the chance to practice being a nonasshole for once. And that's not nothing.

It's the same with our proverbial atheist in philosophy class: Chances are the guy doesn't "hate Jesus." Think about it. When was the last time you heard someone say, "Oh man, that *Jesus*! With the whole 'love your neighbor,' 'feed the poor,' 'turn the other cheek' nonsense? I hate that guy!" No, no one hates *that* Jesus. If they hate anyone, it's the fictional, flag-waving Jesus who bequeathed the Constitution to our Founding Fathers on tablets of stone from Mount Rushmore and then left to torture scientists, blow up abortion clinics, and found the NRA. That's the Jesus they hate. And you know what? I hate him too, and the sooner my hostile classmate knows that, the better. After all, it's often idols that create atheists. What I mean is, it is usually some weird, homespun, politically partisan version of God that occasions the mockery and suspicion toward Christianity that is so rampant in our culture. Outspoken liberal and opponent of (what many consider) Christianity, Bill Maher, provides a perfect example of what I'm talking about:

> Martin Luther King gets to call himself a Christian because he actually practiced loving his enemies. And Gandhi was so fucking Christian, he was Hindu. But, if you rejoice in revenge, torture, and war, . . . you cannot say you're a follower of the guy who explicitly said, "Love your enemies and do good to those who hate you." . . . Really, it's in that book you hold up when you scream at gay people. And, not to put too fine a point on it, but nonviolence was kind of Jesus's trademark. Kind of his big thing. To not follow that part of it is like joining Greenpeace and hating whales. . . .
>
> And, Christians, I know, I'm sorry; I know you hate this and you want to square this circle, but you can't. I'm not even judging you. I'm just saying, logically, if you ignore every single thing Jesus commanded you to do, you're not a Christian. You're just auditing. You're not Christ's followers. You're just fans.

And if you believe the earth was given to you to kick ass on while gloating, you're not really a Christian; you're a Texan.[2]

Rather than getting all butthurt and defensive whenever some imaginary Jesus gets mocked in the culture or the classroom, we would do better to relax, unclench, and join in the laughter. After all, it's no skin off my back when someone dismisses the idea that the earth is six thousand years old, and I have no dog in the whole Adam-rode-to-church-on-a-dinosaur race. The farther I can distance myself from that silliness, the better.

But again, it's not solely a negative thing, as though our entire job is to quarantine ourselves from all the kooks and wackjobs out there. We need to find positive common ground with that atheist, whatever it may be. Does he have compassion for the poor and needy? Is he in love with someone? Is he distraught over police violence against minorities? Does he think the Kardashians are pointless? Any of these could be touchstones to connect on a level that his worldview may not be able to explain but that he may nonetheless appreciate on a deeper level.

Personally, this is something I've been learning through my podcast, *Drunk Ex-Pastors*. My cohost, Christian Kingery,

---

2. *Real Time with Bill Maher*, HBO, May 13, 2011, http://www.hbo.com/real-time-with-bill-maher/episodes/0/213-episode/article/new-rules.html.

is not only an agnostic (and former pastor like me), but he has also been my best friend for the last twenty years. The idea for the show was originally my brother Justin's—we were surfing one day, and he said, "You guys have such interesting discussions when no one's around. You should record them and put them out there and see what happens." I put the idea to Christian (well, I actually just told him that we would be doing a podcast from then on), and the response has been remarkable. Our conversations are literally identical to the ones we have when we're not miked, and the topics we explore range from the existence of God to the problem of evil, from presidential politics to how irritating Justin Bieber's continued existence is (and everything in between). We have listeners around the world, and the constant refrain we hear from our fans goes something like this: "You guys always seem to broach the very topics I have often wanted to discuss but have never felt safe to, and the way you interact (despite your serious differences) is refreshing for its respectfulness, charity, and humor." In other words, what people find unique about what we do is that we are able to model a mutual respect for the other amid our inevitable disagreements, and we have found a way to do it in such a way as to not alienate the 50 percent of our audience that thinks one of us is wrong at any given moment.

Now, obviously Christian's and my long-lasting friendship helps (as does the fact that we open the show by doing a shot and continue to imbibe throughout it). But camaraderie and libations aside, if only those we deem different or "other" could see us dignify their supposed strangeness and show genuine interest in what makes them tick, it would go a long way toward mitigating the ick factor they experience when they think about Christianity. Indeed, if we want to be in step with the gospel and God's plan for humanity, we really don't have a choice.

"No Fight Left, or So It Seems"

In leaving behind the hopelessly fragmented religious tradition of my past and embracing a measure of ambiguity and uncertainty about myself and my positions, I've noticed that I no longer feel the need to fight, win arguments, hunt heretics, or be threatened by the other. Even in writing these things, I don't really care that much if anyone agrees with me or embraces what I'm saying. The things I'm recounting about my own life, and the effects these changes have had upon my broader spiritual journey, are true (at least in my experience). And I can honestly say that it is refreshing not to eye-roll so often or be so ready to dismiss someone's spiritual claims or reflections when they don't comport with my theology as precisely as I demand. People can tell when we're slow-blinking at them, they sense our suspicion, they can tell when we're just waiting for them to shut up so that we can start talking. I don't want to be like that anymore, but would rather heed James's instruction to be "quick to hear, slow to speak" (1:19). But the biggest obstacle to that kind of dignifying treatment of others is thinking you're right and acting like it. Hence a healthy dose of agnosticism here and there can really work wonders for not being such a prick.

Foiled Again!

"Choose your enemies carefully, because they will define you," sings U2's Bono in the song "Cedars of Lebanon." He continues: "When the story ends, they're going to last with you longer than your friends." There's a lot of wisdom there. The sentiment reminds me of (what I consider to be) the greatest program in the history of television: HBO's *The Wire*. The show's main character is Detective Jimmy Mc-Nulty (played by Dominic West), a self-described "murder police" whose dedication to stopping Baltimore's drug violence almost matches his love for Jameson (and his disdain for Bushmills, which he dismisses as "Protestant whiskey"). Throughout the first several seasons of the show, McNulty's arch-nemeses are the members of the Barksdale drug crew and Russell "Stringer" Bell in particular (played masterfully by Idris Elba). Although McNulty and Stringer share only a small handful of scenes together, the latter is never far from the former's mind. What is especially interesting is when— I'd say "spoiler alert," but the show is over a decade old by now—Stringer is murdered by rival gangsters, just as Mc-Nulty acquires the evidence he needs to bust him. While he should be elated at the downfall of his enemy, instead he's just annoyed. He says to his partner, while Stringer's dead body lies a few feet away: "I caught him, Bunk. On the wire, I caught him. And he doesn't fucking know it." When the detectives eventually search Stringer's home, McNulty is even more irritated. Instead of some squalid drug den, he finds a posh modern appointment complete with fine art and a library that includes Adam Smith's classic treatise on the free market, *The Wealth of Nations*. McNulty looks around, puzzled, and mutters under his breath, "Who the fuck was I chasing?"

To the degree we define ourselves against some enemy or foil—be it a person or ideology—to that extent we will never really get around to figuring out who we truly are when we're all alone. Now, don't get me wrong, foils can be useful (although with all due respect to Jimmy Fallon, I can't stand them on late-night talk shows), but many believers—especially professional apologists—need enemies against which to define themselves lest they find themselves out of work: without loony Pentecostals, most Baptists would struggle to figure out who to make fun of; without idolatrous Catholics, many fundamentalists would have trouble figuring out who to populate hell with; and so on.

The problem with this obsessive need for a foil is that such self-identification is by definition negative. In other words, when our entire understanding of who we *are* is shaped by who we *aren't* (which at the end of the day is just xenophobia), we are in an inherently unhealthy place. In such cases, we spend precious little time cultivating a positive identity characterized by the principles and virtues we value, and instead we sit around bitching and moaning about all the lazy Mexicans, bleeding-heart liberals, and right-wing gun nuts out there. (And how they must. Be. Stopped.) When we find ourselves in this type of dynamic, the worst outcome possible is victory. Think about it: If we deport all the "illegals" or successfully ban all the guns, what then? If our entire identity revolves around the dreaded other, his demise will only spell our own. I'm reminded of that brilliant sequence in the movie *Forrest Gump* in which the main character (played by Tom Hanks) is trying to work through some personal issues, and in order to do so he just starts running. (In his own words, "I jus' felt like runnin'.") Pretty soon he starts attracting a massive following of thirsty and confused seekers who are certain that Forrest has the answers they are looking for. (He doesn't, of course—his IQ hovers right around 70.) So Forrest runs and runs and runs some more. At a certain point in the film his running accomplishes its therapeutic aims, so he stops in midstride. His followers, now numbering in the dozens and even hundreds, also stop running, and a hush falls over them: "Shhhh! He's going to say something," one of them announces. At this point Forrest just turns to face them and says, "I'm . . . pretty tired. I think I'll go home now." "Great," one devotee mutters sarcastically. "Now what are we supposed to do?"

When, as a barely-hanging-on pastor, I started surrendering my need to always be right about everything, I pondered what would happen if everyone suddenly decided they agreed with me: What if I got everything I wanted? What if all the Catholics suddenly repented of their horrible idolatry, and all the Baptists started baptizing their babies, and all the Episcopalians jettisoned their wishy-washy limp liberalism? What if all our Calvinistic demands were fully met? I mean, we've been holding Christianity hostage for half a millennium—what if it worked and we actually won? My best guess is that we would then turn on one another and find ways to divide over the various minutiae that we now claim unites us ("Oh, you baptize by sprinkling rather than pouring? Enjoy hell," and so on). You get the point: Being so accustomed to a negative self-identity can leave a massive void when we run out of people to wage doctrinal jihad against.

An Ironic Humility

The brand of Protestantism I avowed was by definition negative—in its rawest form, it was characterized by a protest against what came before and insisted that the errors of the Church were so deal-breaking that we had no choice but to stand apart in marked objection. Yet as I grew more and more accustomed to the Catholic lenses through which I began to behold the world, I noticed something remarkable taking place in me: I lost my lust for theological debate. I know I've hinted at this already, but someone like me ceasing to relish in sparring over biblical exactitude is no small change—it's more like a revolution. For as long as I can remember, I have enjoyed nothing more than debating how-many-angels-can-dance-on-the-head-of-a-pin types of questions. (I remember sitting in a Mexican restaurant in Budapest with a few other pastors, asking them how, if there is no temporal passage of sequential moments in heaven, the "river of life" can be said to "flow" in the age to come. God, I'm annoying.) But that desire for debate waned to the point where I now have almost zero patience for it. Seriously, *I don't really care if people think I'm right anymore.* After leaving my ministry and becoming a kind of misfit civilian, I experienced the dissolving of any and all desire to chest-thump, flex my ecclesial muscles, justify my choice, or prove others wrong.

As I pondered the about-face I was experiencing, I started to realize that whatever humility I now exhibited regarding my own Christian identity was, ironically enough, directly tied to the seemingly audacious self-understanding of the Catholic Church. In a word, the bolder the claims of the Church, the meeker I felt myself becoming. As long as I saw my denomination as being in sibling rivalry with all the others for our Father's attention, it made sense to squabble, to act out, and to jockey for position. But when I found myself in a Church that wasn't a splinter group but the Mother from whom all those siblings had split, well, the desire for one-upmanship pretty much vanished. The claim was no longer "We are the denomination you should choose, and you should consider us because we are the most relevant, most biblically faithful, most family-oriented," or whatever other criteria appeal to ecclesial consumers. On the contrary, the claim of the Church should go something like this: "We are the Church that has always been here, warts and all. And we realize that we will never appeal to every single believer or be able to conform ourselves to the myriad individual demands out there. So we will just keep doing what we're doing while letting people know that our doors are wide open and you're always welcome at any time. And by the way, God loves you regardless of where you worship, and so do we."

In a twisted kind of way, this high-road approach reminds me of one of my all-time favorite TV comedies, *Arrested Development* (albeit by way of counterexample). The show revolves around the Bluths, a wealthy and hilariously corrupt family of real estate developers in Orange County, California. Each character brings his or her own unique brand of eccentric selfishness to the screen, but the family's matriarch, Lucille, takes the proverbial cake. A constant practitioner of passive-aggressive manipulation, Lucille has mastered the art of exploiting her grown children's insecurities to get what she wants. Whether it's mocking her daughter's social life ("Oh, you have the afternoon free? Did 'Nothing' cancel?") or smothering the thirtysomething "baby" of the family ("Buster has become *impossible* to control. Suddenly he's too much of a big-shot to brush Mother's hair"), Lucille's behavior clearly demonstrates that she is no more mature than her children and is in many ways far less so.

How does this apply to my own spiritual journey? What I eventually discovered was that, rather than set herself up as a rival sibling alongside the other claimants to the Best Church Ever title, the Catholic Church understands herself to be the New Eve and therefore "the mother of all living" and "the Mother of us all" (Gen. 3:20; Gal. 4:26, NKJV). Tripping over the arrogance of these self-applied labels might make you miss the humility. How do loving mothers differ from rival siblings? The answer is obvious: Rival siblings claw, scratch, and fight for what they feel is theirs. They posture and seek to carve out for themselves as much space or notoriety or favor as they possibly can. But the mother of rival siblings—does she engage on that level? On the contrary, a caring mother seeks only to exhibit patience toward her warring children and create a safe context in which they can come together and be reconciled. Unlike Lucille Bluth, she does not stoop to their juvenile station but seeks to rise above it and embody a better way. The Catholic Church, at least on her best days and in her best epochs, seeks to be just this for all followers of Jesus: a Mother whose arms are open, whose heart bleeds with love, and whose parameters are less like the walls of a prison than like the borders of a playground. And if I am to mirror this, I must also be open-minded, openhearted, and not only willing but happy to look for the commonality that will unite me with my brothers and sisters rather than getting distracted by the differences that divide us.

Embracing Our Inner Dickhead

"What people are doing when they're forming a band," suggested the famed musician and producer Brian Eno, "is they're forming what an anthropologist would call a clan. It's a group of people who may not be genetically related, but who share interests of some kind. . . . Most of the identity of that group is formed by its separateness from everybody else." To say the various sects within Protestantism are "tribal" is certainly not a stretch, and that was certainly the case with me as a Presbyterian (as I have described already at length). Yet this new "ironic humility" has encouraged me to set aside the bloodlust and open the door to forge a positive self-identity rather than a solely negative one. When you no longer need a foil, when you cease seeing yourself or your group as doctrinal watchdogs or the antidote to some prior problem, you can finally start asking "What do I affirm?" instead of dwelling on "What do I deny?" And trust me, this is way harder than it sounds. Anyone can be anti-: Politicians can be anti-guns or anti-abortion, sociologists can be anti-porn or anti-abstinence-only sex ed, the public can be anti-vaccinations or anti-GMOs. But to turn from what we are *against* and think about what we are *for* is another matter altogether. It takes a bit of soul-searching and a whole lot of creativity and original thinking.

In this connection I can't help but think back to my first few weeks of high school. Many of my fellow freshmen—kids I had known since elementary school—showed up on

game days with their football jerseys or cheerleading uni-
forms on. I had stopped playing team sports a couple of
years earlier and spent my free time surfing and skateboard-
ing, and I had a bit of a dismissive attitude toward these
jocks: "Oh, for crying out loud, could you *be* any more of a
cliché? You people even have your own table in the quad!"
The way high school works is that certain people choose
their clique, while the leftovers wind up in random associa-
tions by default. To invoke the categories from *Ferris Bueller's
Day Off,* the "sportos" may be sportos by choice, and the
same may be true of the "motorheads," but what about the
"geeks, sluts, bloods, wastoids, dweebies, and dickheads"?
It's easy to define yourself according to what you're *not* (and
even easier to let yourself be so defined by others), but knowing what you *are* is a much rarer thing indeed.

While we're on the topic of iconic 1980s high-school-
themed films, I would be remiss if I didn't mention *The
Breakfast Club.* If you haven't seen this brilliant exposé of
teenage clique culture, you should just put this book down
right now and go watch it. Seriously, I won't be offended. But
in case it has been a while, I'll remind you of the plot. Five
high school students, for various reasons, are sentenced to
spend an entire Saturday in detention for their misdeeds at
school. The biggest challenge of the day is not the detention
itself but who it is spent with. You see, none of these five
students would likely ever associate with one another during normal school hours since they run in differing circles
(or in none at all). But as the day wears on, their masks

are lowered and their forced and extraneous personas begin to melt away, revealing the real person beneath. And here's the really interesting part. The teacher assigned to supervise them tells them to write a thousand-word essay explaining "who you think you are," but the detainees decide to ignore the assignment, and instead leave for him a letter that simply reads:

> *Dear Mr. Vernon,*
>
> *We accept the fact that we had to sacrifice a whole Saturday in detention for whatever it was we did wrong, but we think you're crazy to make us write an essay telling you who we think we are. What do you care? You see us as you want to see us. In the simplest terms, and most convenient definitions, you see us as a brain, an athlete, a basket case, a princess, and a criminal. Does that answer your question?*
>
> *Sincerely yours,*
>
> *The Breakfast Club*

Few people realize that this letter is read both at the very beginning of the film and the very end, and the two versions are slightly different, but the difference is incredibly significant. In the initial version (reflected above), the identities of the students are presented through the lens of Mr. Vernon's simplistic perception of them: "You see us as x, y, and z." But after the day has ended and the masks have been painfully torn off, the letter reflects the students' new awareness that they have much more in common than the strict high school social rules allowed them to recognize. "What we found out," the final version of the letter says, "is that *each one of us* is a brain, and an athlete, a basket case, a princess, and a criminal." In other words, each student has taken a piece of the others with them and will carry it around forever, despite the fact that some admit that they will not acknowledge the others when Monday rolls around.

Like it or not, we are all connected. Not long after the tragic shooting of unarmed Florida teenager Trayvon Martin by George Zimmerman, a slogan spread across various social media platforms: "I Am Trayvon Martin." It attempted to express that we are all potential victims of xenophobia, fear, and the violence they incite. We're all a minority somewhere (and you may be one where you live), and the sooner we recognize the dangers of mistrusting the dreaded "other," the closer we will be to actually living in a society in which dozens of people aren't gunned down in mass shootings every month. (Hey, a guy can dream, right?) So yes, I'm Trayvon Martin. I'm each of the victims of the Orlando shooting at the Pulse nightclub in June 2016 (which at this writing is the largest mass shooting in America's history but may be superseded before this book is published). I am the stranger. I am my enemy, for I share something in common with him that is deeper than what divides us: human nature. The brain is also an athlete, the dweebie is also a dickhead, and the princess is also a criminal. "Each one of us is."

Embracing this truth has been one of the most liberating things in my life. Now when I encounter someone foreign or strange to me, my propensity to lock in on how we are different is slowly being eclipsed by the tendency to seek out our similarities and sameness (and to learn from how we differ, since they might be strong where I am weak). Far from providing me with occasions to distinguish myself, Catholicism has provided me with a touchstone of connection and commonality with others: "You have priests? We have priests too!" "You have altars? So do we!" "You revere nature and exalt the earth? We do as well, and we even see the divinity in created things!" Here's my point: It's not hard to find common ground with people of other religious or cultural backgrounds, and a *"You* like pizza? *I* like pizza!" approach to life is far healthier than one whose default posture is "You're doing it wrong."

This approach to life is necessarily vulnerable, because it opens us up to self-examination and the possibility of being overly narrow or even mistaken about things. The fact is that the world is much smaller than it used to be, and discovering differing perspectives is much simpler. If Catholicism is truly "catholic" (which means "universal" and comes from the Greek phrase meaning "according to the whole"), then we should look upon the ability to encounter new perspectives as welcome and fortuitous rather than scary. I would prefer to learn—and even to learn that I'm wrong—than be so circumspect that I'm constantly walking on eggshells or tiptoeing around viewpoints that differ from my own. As our world shrinks and our borders become more fluid, it's all too easy to retreat into our insulated bunkers and familiar, fortified ghettoes. But to do so would be to miss far too many opportunities to learn and be stretched. I mean, what if the guy with the curly sidelocks and yarmulke has something to teach me about fearless discipline and devotion? What if the woman with dreadlocks protesting Monsanto knows something about the politics of food that I've not yet learned? Sure, the former may be a bit austere and the latter may have too much pit hair and BO, but so what? I'd rather endure a bit of discomfort and odor than spend my life in some pitiful circle-jerk, an echo chamber filled with nodding avatars of myself.

Embracing and embodying a misfit faith is not about seeing the light, patting ourselves on the back, and making converts. (Plus, is there some "light" we're supposed to see, really? So much of our experience of the real world feels more like twilight than some binary choice between good guys in white hats or bad guys in black ones.) Being a misfit means discovering that a lack of curiosity about the other is not a virtue but a vice and an ugly one at that. Indeed, misfit faith is all about being okay with being wrong. And the nice thing about being wrong once is that it liberates us to do it again.

5

Shit Happens

(Or, The Excruciating Disruption of Power)

How to Keep Your Marbles

If ever there was a perfect embodiment of the thirst for power, it would have to be Jack Donaghy, Alec Baldwin's character on the TV show *30 Rock*. Set at a fictional version of NBC, the program focuses on the network's *Saturday Night Live*–style late-night comedy show. Jack is head of the studio and is therefore in charge of all contract negotiations with the program's actors—an aspect of his job that he, as a rabid capitalist, absolutely relishes. In one scene, Jack is discussing the expiring contract of Josh, one of the show's main actors, with a colleague. He insists that Josh is replaceable and that during negotiations he must be treated as an enemy: "Josh is going to try to grab all the marbles, and it is our job to hide them." When his colleague points out that that is not how you play marbles, Jack's response is "But that's how you *keep* them." When the initial negotiations are about to take place, Jack invites Josh and his agent to sit down, but the chairs provided for them are ridiculously low to the ground, giving Jack a psychological edge. (In the second meeting, he again motions for them to sit, but there are no chairs at all!) Jack understands better than most that getting ahead in life (and especially in business) necessarily involves taking advantage of others' weaknesses and using every inch of ground as leverage to gain a little more, until he has all the proverbial marbles. In a word, it's all about exploitation and control.

We see this pretty much everywhere we look. In race and gender relations, the group that has more political and financial power can wield it to their advantage by creating laws or employing double standards to further marginalize those in the minority. (We have a long way to go to right these wrongs, but things are slowly improving.) The power dynamic is also at work in individual relationships: when a guy remarks to a girl at a club that her shoes look comfortable or the dress she's wearing looks great on her body type, he's intending to gain a psychological edge by confusing her about whether he just complimented or insulted her. That despicable practice perfectly exemplifies the way power can function in our lives.

Many pastors play the power game by comparing the size of their congregations with those of their fellow ministers (and the larger the congregation, often the larger the paycheck). My point is that the lure of earthly power is great, and the lust for it spans just about every facet of life. In this chapter, though, I hope to set forth a very different perspective on power, one that is shaped not by greed and the lust for wealth or greatness, but by self-emptying and sacrifice.

God the Great and Powerful

Where does God fit into all this? It may seem that of all the culprits in the power game, God is the most egregious offender. Think about it: He is by definition "all powerful," and he isn't satisfied with mere omnipotence but demands the unceasing adoration of all people everywhere and at all times. Basically, to hear his detractors tell it, he is the consummate cosmic narcissist who spends all day looking at himself in the mirror primping and taking selfies. In a word, God is part Kanye and part Kardashian. And it's not like his followers haven't left behind a consistent track record reinforcing this very idea. Whether we're talking about slavery, the oppression of women, or economic injustice, it has all been justified by the so-called faithful under the guise of divine precedent, manifest destiny, the Puritan work ethic, or whatever other insidious label you can find littering the history of the Western world.

This was brought home to me in a Facebook meme I saw the other day that said something like "God only knocks you down to get you to look up." It seems somewhat innocuous at first, until it just doesn't. The underlying message is

"God is too much of a gentleman to intervene in your life without your consent. So he'll just keep beating the shit out of you until your permission is extracted." Sounds a bit like that "enhanced interrogation" we employ with terrorists: They may not be willing to cooperate, but don't worry, we'll *make* them willing.

But as I have argued, God is not petty. He does not pine after power the way we often do, or exert his strength in order to exploit the weak and maximize his own gains. How do we know this? Is there some way to determine what this remote and unknowable deity is really like? Thankfully, the answer is yes, and it's surprisingly simple.[1] Consider these three passages from the New Testament:

> Philip said to [Jesus], "Lord, show us the Father, and it is enough for us." Jesus said to him, "Have I been with you so long, and you still do not know me, Philip? Whoever has seen me has seen the Father." (John 14:8–9)

> [Christ] is the image of the invisible God. . . . For in him all the fullness of God was pleased to dwell. (Col. 1:15, 19)

> [Jesus] is the radiance of the glory of God and the exact imprint of his nature. (Heb. 1:3)

---

1. I am indebted to Bradley Jersak and his book *A More Christlike God: A More Beautiful Gospel* (Pasadena, CA: Plain Truth Ministries, 2015) for much of the insight that follows.

If we want to know what God is like, and especially how divine power functions, we can simply look at Jesus. As the passages above point out, seeing Jesus is seeing the Father, for he is the visible image of God and the *icon* and perfect representation of God's personality. What, then, was Jesus like during his earthly ministry? Let's briefly examine a few accounts from the gospels to gain a clear idea.

The most obvious place to start would be his birth. As Matthew and Luke both indicate, the circumstances surrounding the birth of Christ were far from ideal, beginning with a long and difficult journey by his earthly father and very pregnant mother, not to mention a less-than-comfortable (and far less-than-hygienic) delivery room: basically a stable filled with all the sounds, smells, and waste that you would expect from such a place. But setting aside the physical surroundings of Jesus's birth, consider the fact that God the Son, the second Person of the Holy Trinity, stooped so low as to consent to actual childbirth in the first place! To assume human nature with all its weaknesses and limitations, to further experience the helplessness of an infant, and to place himself under the care and authority of earthly parents are all sublime examples of the lengths to which the Son of God was willing to go in order to reach mankind with the message of divine love.

The second place to look is a story in which some members of the religious establishment drag a woman before Jesus whom they claim was caught in the act of adultery (John 8:1–11). They put forth the challenge, "In the Law

Moses commanded us to stone such women. So what do you say?" Jesus's response was to ignore them completely, stooping down and doodling in the dirt with his finger. Once the religious leaders got tired of waiting for an answer and left, Jesus said to the woman, "Woman, where are they?" meaning her accusers. "Has no one condemned you?" When she answered, "No one," Jesus responded, "And neither do I condemn you; go, and from now on sin no more."

Our third look at the life of Jesus features an expert in God's law coming to him and asking him which of all the 613 moral, civil, and ceremonial commands in God's law was the most important (Mark 12:28–34). Jesus answered, in effect, "Love God with all you are—heart, soul, mind, and strength, and love your neighbor as yourself." The scribe replied that he agreed, and that surely love of God and neighbor outweighed all religious rites and ceremonies, to which Jesus responded, "You are not far from the kingdom of God."

What do these few brief accounts show us? While much more could be said and many more examples adduced, we can see very clearly from these episodes that Jesus was humble and self-emptying, that he was compassionate and quick to forgive, and that he valued love over ritual and pomp. After all, he could have entered our world with displays of magnificence and splendor, he could have slut-shamed the adulterous woman and green-lit her execution, and he could have told the inquisitive scribe something like "Nice try, but prioritizing God's commands will just make you ne-

glect the silly ones about your clothing and diet, so just quit being a sniveling baby and keep them all." But instead of taking the low road, Jesus chose the "more excellent way" of mercy and love. Now, my point in bringing all this up, in case you haven't figured it out yet, is that if the passages I cited from John, Colossians, and Hebrews are to be taken seriously, then God is exactly like Jesus. God is humble and self-emptying, God's default mode is forgiveness and non-condemnation, and God is more concerned with love than with law.

Returning to our main topic, how does this all relate to the issue of power? By now the answer should be obvious: God doesn't "do control" the way our culture teaches us to think about it. Is God "omnipotent," as Bible scholars suggest? Of course. But that's not the question. The real question is how that power is exercised, and if God is just like Jesus, the answer is that God exercises his power in a way that is *kenotic* and *cruciform*. Now, if you're a normal person and not some theology nerd, you'll need those terms defined, and to do that, let's turn to the episode that above all others shows us what Jesus, and therefore God, is really like.

Kenotic and Cruciform Power

As I said above, God exhibits his power ever and only in ways that are kenotic and cruciform. The latter term simply means "shaped and formed by the cross," meaning that whenever God exercises his power, he does so in a way that mirrors the self-giving and sacrificial love displayed by Jesus on Calvary. This brings us to the term *kenotic*, which comes from the Greek word used in Philippians 2:7 to refer to Jesus having "emptied himself" by his humble submission to the crucifixion. The passage reads:

> Have this mind among yourselves, which is yours in Christ Jesus, who, though he was in the form of God, did not count equality with God a thing to be grasped, but emptied himself, by taking the form of a servant, being born in the likeness of men. And being found in human form, he humbled himself by becoming obedient to the point of death, even death on a cross. Therefore God has highly exalted him and bestowed on him the name that is above every name, so that at the name of Jesus every knee should bow, in heaven and on earth and under the earth, and every tongue confess that Jesus Christ is Lord, to the glory of God the Father. (Philippians 2:5–11)

While many read this passage and conclude that the Son's earthly life and death represented a mere temporary dipping of the divine toe into the waters of self-giving and sacrifice, I think much more is being said here. If God is exactly like Jesus, then what the Son exhibited throughout his whole earthly life—and especially on the cross—was not just sacrificial self-giving love but also a sneak peek behind the veil at the very character of his Father. As we discussed earlier, a Father is what God is, and fatherhood is what God does. From all eternity, God has been fathering a divine family; he has been reproducing his own image in his Son, meaning that the dynamic of self-giving is not just something Jesus displayed for a short while during his earthly ministry; it characterizes the relationship of the Father to the Son as well. In a word, by his own cruciform example of sacrificial and self-emptying love, the Son of God gave us a glimpse of the mutually self-giving love of the Father. (And as the passage makes plain, the Father approved of the Son's illustration of divine love as evidenced by his raising him from the dead.)

When Christ submitted to the constant attacks of the religious elite, he was showing us what God is like. When he "opened not his mouth," refusing to utter a word of self-defense before his accusers, he was mirroring the character of God. When he surrendered to the abject cruelty of his "crowning" and consented to Roman crucifixion (from which word we derive the term *excruciating*), he was divulging more about what God is like than all the Old Testament stories combined.

I'll take this a step further. The more I journey along this path—seeing God as loving, unifying, and, well, fatherly—the more convinced I become that any biblical account that describes God in a non-Christlike way simply must be treated with extreme care and nuance. To illustrate this with a touch of humor, I do a segment on my *Drunk Ex-Pastors* podcast called "Dick Move, God," in which I embody a biblical character and lament my life's circumstances to my cohost, Christian (who's an agnostic, as you know already, and doesn't know which character I have chosen beforehand). An example from a recent episode went something like this:

"Man, I'm totally bummed out, I just returned from my son's funeral."

"Oh no, I'm so sorry," he replied. "What happened?"

"Well from what I have been able to piece together," I began, "my son was at the market when this guy Samson showed up. Apparently—and the details are still a bit sketchy—this Samson character had made a bet with these thirty guys that if they guessed the answer to a riddle, he told them he would provide each of them with a change of clothes. Well, I guess Samson's wife pressured him into telling her the answer, and then she went and divulged it to the thirty men. But instead of just ponying up the agreed-upon reward, Samson decided to murder thirty *other* guys, take *their* clothes, and pay off the men he made the bet with. And one of them was my son. So he's dead now, all because this douchebag Samson didn't feel like honoring his own idiotic bet that he lost fair and square."

"Well," my cohost replied, seeking to console me, "you can't really blame God for what Samson did, can you?"

"You'd think not," I answered. "But it turns out—and here's the real sucker punch—it was the 'Spirit of God' who came upon him and *enabled* him to brutally murder my son and the rest of the victims to pay his debt. Pretty dick move, if you ask me. Now, I have no son, and there's some lunatic running around ready to slaughter people for personal gain, who's got an all-powerful God in his corner who's apparently ready to be his accomplice. There goes the neighborhood."

Now, I know what you're thinking: "How can you say such a thing, calling God's actions a 'dick move'? Isn't this tantamount to blasphemy?" A fair question, but by this point I hope the answer is clear. If God is just like Jesus, then the real question is "Would Jesus have done this? Would Jesus have been an accomplice to ː ˙ murder of thirty random innocent people in order that th ː˙ loodstained clothes could be taken off their dead corpses anu given to thirty other men to whom some asinine bet had been lost?" I trust the answer is obvious, but in case it isn't, it's no, Jesus wouldn't help his so-called anointed servant brutally slaughter a bunch of guys for any reason, let alone one as preposterous as this. Indeed, to turn the issue around, it seems to me more "blasphemous" to suggest that God *would* do such a thing than that he *wouldn't*.

So what do we do with accounts in the Bible that depict God as some sort of foaming-at-the-mouth maniac? To be honest, I have no idea. I'll leave that to the professional theologians and scholars of Scripture (which thankfully I no longer am!). Suffice it to say that I have abandoned the kind of good cop/bad cop paradigm according to which at any moment God can just flip out and go postal on a person or group of people for no good reason. And call me self-congratulatory, but I'm pretty sure God agrees with me on this one.

Returning to my main point, then, the God that I have discovered is one whose power is never exercised except in ways that are self-emptying and consistent with Christ's sacrificial death on the cross. Divine omnipotence is always coupled with divine consent both to our human free will and to the laws of nature. This means that God doesn't "do power" in a manner that does violence to our choices or to the way the world naturally works.

Now, this way of understanding God has huge ramifications for our everyday lives, especially when we suffer. For example, how many times have you heard objections like "How could a loving God give people cancer?" It's a really good question, and while the ultimate response needs to involve a serious dose of agnosticism and humility at the prospect of defending God or speaking on his behalf, the things we are discussing can actually be helpful here. If God doesn't throw his omnipotent weight around or constantly interrupt human free will, then the notion that God "gives people cancer" is severely fallacious. I'm reminded of a comic strip that shows a man lying in a hospital bed while his doctor tells him that although he has cancer, it is all a part of God's plan. The next panel shows God up in heaven making a to-do list that reads, "1. Create world; 2. Give Carl cancer; 3. _____." The obvious joke is that God is just shooting from the hip and flying by the seat of his pants, randomly doling out pestilence and plague, and then trying to decide whether to solve the problems he causes.

But according to the understanding of God that I have begun to embrace, God didn't give Carl cancer at all. Carl got cancer probably as the natural effect of some prior cause, like eating processed food or living near a cell tower. In order to blame God for someone getting cancer, then, you also have to blame God for letting that person eat Twinkies and use an iPhone. Imagine a world in which no one contracted cancer because every potentially cancer-causing activity that we freely desired to engage in was off-limits. And taking it a step further, does God give football players concussions, drown surfers, or snap snowboarders' legs? Of course not, but he does allow people to engage in activities that may cause those kinds of deaths or injuries. Is God to blame for that? When a skydiver's parachute fails to open, is God the one who hurled the guy to the earth? I trust you're getting my point, which is that God's involvement in this world—especially the way he exercises power—is by self-emptying nonviolent consent. And nothing illustrates this dynamic more beautifully than the cross, at which the Son demonstrated not only his utter and complete participation in human suffering, but also his unwillingness to intervene in and disrupt the evil devices of wicked men.

While this version of divine omnipotence isn't nearly as ballsy as that of the Calvinist God (who foreordains horrific evils such as rape because "how dare you question *me*!"), maybe it's time to jettison that entire masculine, muscle-flexing view of God anyway. (And while I'm on the subject, since when did testicles become the symbol of toughness? They're like the most sensitive things ever.) As long as we demand an airtight theology with a well-behaved God, we'll be able to cavalierly answer all of life's tough questions, despite coming off as total assholes: "9/11? That was the gays' fault." "Katrina? Blame the hedonists in New Orleans." "Earthquake in Haiti? Payback for voodoo witch doctors" (all of which were actually suggested as reasons for these tragic events by Christian leaders at the time). But when we adopt a theology with a healthy measure of messiness and ambiguity thrown in, the seeming weakness on God's part will be a small price to pay if (1) we don't make God out to be a maniacal control freak, and (2) Jesus dies on a cross. Sacred weakness is greater than secular strength, is what I'm saying.

So the next time we are confronted with someone who has faced a serious calamity and sees it as a justifiable reason to hate God, perhaps we should check ourselves before heartlessly entering into that clinical and dismissive "apologetics mode" according to which we smugly say things like "Oh, you lost your only child in a freak blimp accident at the state fair on the same day your wife left you and your parents both died of mad cow disease? Well as the Bible says, God works in mysterious ways. Plus, you deserve much worse since you failed to praise him enough that one time, so consider yourself lucky." I'll go out on a limb here and suggest that if you are ever tempted to actually say things like this—

even if more mildly and less over-the-top, I mean—then you make Jesus sad. I'm sorry, but the fact of the matter is that shit happens and life can suck sometimes. And when things get bad, it can feel like *if* there were an omnimalevolent Being with enough malice and power to ruin, damage, and dupe us into thinking that we will finally reap in joy what we have sown in tears, that spiteful god couldn't do a better job of executing his twisted plan than by simply copying what the "good" God often puts us through. Indeed, "if at all God's gaze upon us falls, it's with a mischievous grin."[2]

Perhaps a better response to those who claim to hate God is something like "Yeah, me too sometimes." After all, if there is one thing the Bible makes clear, it's that the opposite of faith is not doubt—it is sight (2 Cor. 5:7). This means that faith is best exercised when it seems like God is an absentee landlord or deadbeat dad. Yes, he is an eternal Father, as I have been arguing. But as I have also been arguing, God's interaction with us in this age is modeled after the cross, the episode that above all others shows not only his co-suffering love but also his willingness to allow human beings to express their autonomy despite the potentially disastrous effects of their choices both for themselves and for those who follow. After all, it was at Calvary that Jesus described himself as "forsaken" (Matt. 27:46). If the Son of God thought it was okay to display sufficient authenticity and anguish to

---

2. I find myself constantly stealing this line from Dave Matthews's song "Seek Up."

question his Father's inactivity and refusal to rescue, then surely we can too.

Now Is the Gospel of Our Discontent

Let those final couple of sentences sink in. My guess is that the last source we would ever expect for the idea that God "forsakes" people during their most trying times would be Jesus himself, and yet that is exactly what he accused God of doing in his infamous cry of dereliction from the cross, "My God, My God, why have you forsaken me?" This reminds me of a 1998 Point/Counterpoint article from the brilliant satirical newspaper *The Onion*. Playing off the well-known "Footprints in the Sand" Christian inspirational poster, the Point section has Jesus telling Jim Steinhauer that his life, represented by the footprints in the sand, shows only one set of footprints during his most difficult times because "it was then that I carried you." In the Counterpoint section, Jim responds to Jesus by saying, "Bullshit, Jesus, those are obviously my footprints. . . . The only thing I do remember about my worst moments on the path of life is the horrible feeling of plodding along the cold sand all alone while icy rain fell in sheets and chill winds assailed me. So thanks, Jesus. Thanks a bunch. You were really there for me when things got tough. Asshole."

To the theologically uptight, this probably sounds like complete blasphemy, but to the rest of us, it's pretty hilarious. The obvious point is that there are times in our lives when God feels like anything but a "refuge from the storm," a "present help in times of trouble," or any of the other comforting things the Bible says he is supposed to be. But as I've suggested, Jesus himself can relate to that feeling of being forsaken and ignored to a greater degree than we will ever know, and on the cross he wasn't afraid to give expression to it in a way that sounded pretty theologically incorrect. In a word, Jesus was suffering and in pain, and God was nowhere to be found.

Christianity as a kind of panacea and cure-all for every single problem we face is a complete farce. A huge part of the gospel consists of God routinely forsaking us rather than running to our aid and fixing all our boo-boos. In fact, it's precisely the idea that we are *supposed* to feel whole and complete that creates most of our problems and confusion in the first place.[3] Going all the way back to the creation narrative, we find man longing for wholeness and fulfillment—in Adam's case, the fruit of the forbidden tree represented the "sacred object" that would fill his void. The history of humankind ever since has been a quest to discover and seize that longed-for something, that elusive missing piece that will put everything in its right place, dot every i, and cross every t. Some seek it in money, others in fame, and still others in drugs, alcohol, or some relationship or other. But the problem, as most of us know, is that these things—

---

3. I am indebted to the work of philosopher Peter Rollins for much of the insight that follows.

innocuous though they may be in and of themselves—never truly deliver the satisfaction that we expected of them.

Now, at this point your eyes are probably starting to glaze over (at least if you've had some experience in evangelical Christianity). You've been to enough rallies, crusades, and evangelistic meetings to be torturously familiar with this whole spiel: "Are you unhappy? Unfulfilled? Sick and tired of being sick and tired? You feel this way because you've been seeking happiness in all the wrong things," et cetera, et cetera—you know the rest. Here the preacher generally shifts gears and explains that the happiness and wholeness that sinners seek from worldly sources can be found only in Christ and a relationship with him. But here I would demur and explore a very different approach. What if faith is not so much about filling voids and plugging God-shaped holes as about getting to that existential place where we embrace the doubt, complexity, and ambiguity of life in this world? What if Christianity—far from reinforcing the "fulfillment narrative" according to which Jesus (rather than worldly things) satisfies us—actually sets us free from the oppressive notion that anything can? In short, what if the life of faith is a life that accepts just how crappy the life of faith really is? Can it be that sadness is just happiness for deep people?

We see a huge hint at this in the episode we have been discussing: the crucifixion. When Jesus uttered his cry of dereliction, "My God, my God, why have you forsaken me?" something significant took place in the temple in Jerusalem, which was not far from where he was hanging on the cross.

Separating the temple's inner sanctum, or "Holy of Holies," from the rest of the temple was a massive thick veil or curtain. Its purpose was to conceal God's presence and keep sinful people out. No common Israelites were allowed behind the veil; only the High Priest could venture into that inner sanctuary, and only once a year on the Jewish Day of Atonement, in order to offer a holy sacrifice for his own sins and the sins of the people. It was commonly believed that if anyone else ventured behind the veil, or if the High Priest did so in an unworthy manner, the sheer brilliance of God's unmasked and unmitigated presence would immediately put him to death. As in that iconic scene in *Raiders of the Lost Ark* in which Nazis discover and open the Ark of the Covenant and the angel of God's wrath destroys those who dare look (literally melting the skin off their faces), the expectation for any breach of "Holy of Holies protocol" was similarly gruesome and dire.

When Christ uttered his cry, the temple veil was "torn in two, from top to bottom" (Matt. 27:51). And yet nothing happened. No warm glow was emitted, no flood of divine Agent Orange–like pestilence surged to consume the unworthy, no Morgan Freeman–type character with a beard and white robe appeared. Nope, there was nothing there, and none of that stuff transpired.

Returning, then, to what I was hinting at above, I suspect that at least part of the cross's significance lies in the idea that bundled with the death of Jesus is the death of the "sacred object." In other words, the point of the gospel is not that the mysterious and hidden thing that we spend so much time and energy searching for (whatever it may be) will come to us through Jesus, as though we were correct in our search but just using the wrong vending machine. No, on the contrary, the point is that that elusive and potentially satisfying thing that we desire so badly *doesn't exist in the first place*. It is a farce, a sham. This is what philosopher Peter Rollins refers to when he speaks of "the nihilistic heart of Christianity," namely, that the sacred object that always seems just barely beyond our grasp is an idol and an illusion, and that with the death of Christ comes the death of the idea that we can ever obtain the wholeness and satisfaction that we have spent our lives longing for. This is what it means to be "united with [Christ] in [his] death," as Paul says (Rom. 6:5). If the cross is about the forsakenness of Christ, it's about our own forsakenness too.

But there is more to the story (a good thing, because so far this all sounds seriously depressing). Just as Christ was taken away only to return in a new form in the resurrection, so the sacred object dies—at least as an external object and idol that we love and seek—but then returns to us in a new way. Instead of the sacred being some *thing* we strive for to mitigate our sense of brokenness, we now experience it in the midst of that brokenness. Instead of "God" being an extrinsic object that we love, God *is* love, and by loving our neighbor, our enemy, the Other, and the world, we indirectly love God himself. Just as light is not seen but instead provides the means to see, so God is present when love is given and lived out in the midst of all the messiness and complexity of life as we experience it. This is beautifully (and performatively) illustrated in the celebration of the Eucharist: Christ is consumed under the appearance of bread and wine (he "disappears" as he did after his crucifixion), but as in the resurrection, he returns, albeit in a form that is different from the one he had when he left. After Christ is eaten and consumed, he becomes manifest not in the flesh but in the midst of his people who, as his mystical Body, may actually *be* him to the world around them.

When Scripture says, therefore, that "love fulfills the law," it doesn't mean that love is just another requirement that threatens and scares us because we fail to meet it, but rather that love exists on a different plane and a higher register than law ever did. Love is not a super law or a divine doubling-down on the old economy—it is a "new and living way" that has been opened up through the true temple veil, which is the flesh of Christ (Heb. 10:20). Jesus's death, then, is not simply the payment of a debt. It is the obliteration of the system that makes debt possible and gives it its power in the first place. The gospel is not about an angry judge forgiving our sins by venting his fury on an innocent victim—it's about bridging the gap that separated the divine and human, the sacred and secular, by means of a co-suffering God-Man in whose self-giving love we are called to participate. To sum up, it's not about power according to its worldly wielding—

it's about sacrifice, surrender, and the unmixed love of the stranger. It is here, amid these postures and positions, that God is truly found.

Why has all this become so crucial for me? Well, to the degree that God is some object I'm supposed to love more than all the other objects in my life, to that degree I consider myself an utter failure at this whole Christianity thing that I have been pursuing pretty seriously for the last twenty-seven years. Virtually all my attempts at direct devotion to God wind up feeling completely hollow. To quote the late Keith Green, "My eyes are dry, my faith is old, my heart is hard, my prayers are cold." But with that said, I do find myself profoundly moved by other things: the people I love, the art and music and films that tug at this or that facet of my soul, the physical locations that have become sacred spaces for me, and so on. Perhaps it is precisely by embracing human-ity with wholehearted affirmation that we indirectly affirm divinity. Perhaps it is by saying an unequivocal, gut-level yes to earth that we experience heaven. Perhaps (to borrow the German pastor Dietrich Bonhoeffer's suggestion) it is by liv-ing as though God doesn't exist that we finally begin to give him his due. Could it be that we "love God" *by* "loving our neighbor," and that the way to the divine Father is through the flesh of the human Christ?

I sure hope so, because if not I am screwed. . . .

6

Too Good to Be False
(Or, Religion Is a Fairy Tale)

Once Upon a Time

When my oldest daughter, Ainsley, was little, she was really into the Disney princesses. I mean *really* into them: She read all the books, dressed in their clothes, and engaged me in discussions about which princesses were the best. (For the record, it's Belle. And don't get me started on Snow White—she's completely lame. Why she's part of the pantheon while *Enchanted*'s Giselle gets overlooked is beyond me.) For her fourth birthday, she even got to go to Disneyland and attend a special lunch where each of the princesses came to her table. They talked, hugged, and took photos together. As her dad, I think I may have been as excited for her as she was for herself: *Ariel is standing right there! Holy crap! It's really her!*

Since Ainsley left the Disney princess phase, all three of my kids have completely embraced the *Star Wars* universe and mythology (as I have mentioned), and they have more recently become interested in J. R. R. Tolkien's Middle Earth, especially in *The Hobbit* and *Lord of the Rings*. While I didn't read Tolkien until my twenties, I did grow up with Luke Skywalker and the Force, and like most families, mine had our own ways of paying homage to Santa Claus and the Tooth Fairy. (Speaking of the latter, a couple of years ago my daughter Fiona wrote a letter to the Tooth Fairy asking how big she was, and if she could "keep" her. In my response as the Tooth Fairy, using my best cursive, I explained that I am the size of a large butterfly and no, she can't keep me since I have a lot of work still to do.)

While it is easy to dismiss fairy tales as children's fare, the truth is that all people need stories. In fact, the telling of tales resides at the very core of our being and always has. If we were to create a time machine and travel back to the ancient cultures of the past, we would see tribespeople of antiquity gathering around their sacred fires and saying things like "The moon and stars were vomited forth by the god Bumba, ruler of the Bantu tribe" or "The Great Spirit of the Cherokee created the earth by means of Dâyuni'sï, the water beetle." We see a similar appeal to pop folklore in George R. R. Martin's book series *A Song of Ice and Fire* (on which HBO's *Game of Thrones* is based). The story's no-madic and tribal Dothraki people have a phrase that, when uttered, tends to end debate over a subject. The phrase? "It is known." Here's how it works: "The moon is no egg that hatched dragons. The moon is a goddess, the wife of the sun.

It is known." And that's all it takes. If a thing is "known," then *bam,* mic-drop, end of discussion.

What do these old-timey or fictional people have to do with us today? Well, consider another story that has had a pretty significant effect on twenty-first-century Westerners: "In the beginning, [Elohim] created the heavens and the earth . . . and [Elohim] said, 'Let there be light,' and there was light" (Gen. 1:1, 3). Like all the religions surrounding the Israelites, the very Judaism upon which Christianity was founded originated as a story, a myth that mothers and priests and sages would speak with hushed tones and reverence. (And since grace perfects nature, why would we expect any different?) In fact, the founding document and constitution of the ancient Hebrew people (commonly known as the Decalogue or Ten Commandments), begins with a story (what scholars call a Historical Prologue): "I am the Lord your God, who brought you out of the land of Egypt, out of the house of slavery" (Ex. 20:2). In this chapter I'd like to situate ourselves and our individual stories within the larger context of the grander tales we tell and ultimately within the grandest tale of all: the one that God is telling.

Our Narrative Identity

We humans are contextual beings by nature—we self-identify according to stories or narratives that ground who we are. For example, when I meet someone for the first time,

I don't introduce myself by saying, "Hello, I'm Jason. I'm a collection of cells and tissue and bones, and I have a digestive and central nervous system." No, the proper answer to the question "Tell me about yourself?" is something like "Well, I come from California. I have a younger brother. I'm a writer and podcaster, and I currently live in the Seattle area." In short, we answer the question "Who are you?" with what philosophers call narrative discourse: by telling a story. While genetics and biology can relay certain factual data about us, we are more than the sum of our parts. What makes us unique and human is our background, personal history, and lived experiences.

Furthermore, the story we tell is self-authenticating, meaning it doesn't play by the same rules as other kinds of discourse. The statement, for example, that water boils at 212 degrees Fahrenheit is a scientific claim, and as such it is subject to testing, scrutiny, and verification or falsification. Likewise with the claim that President John F. Kennedy was assassinated on November 22, 1963: It is a fact that can be denied, but only ignorantly. (Like water's boiling point, it is true whether we know about it or not.) But narrative discourse operates according to a different language game. When I ground myself in a story (being born when I was, being raised where I was, living where I do), I am saying that who I am is intimately related to my personal narrative, that I am not an isolated disembodied "island" but am an embedded human person with a context that shapes me. When I share that my past experiences contribute to my present fear of trusting people with my inner insecurities, or that being a white male makes it hard for me to recognize abuses of power, I am not inviting rigid scrutiny or wanting those claims put under a microscope and validated. Sure, we should all be open to therapeutic moments of self-discovery and new insight into ourselves, but that only proves my point. While in my smug sure-of-myself days I used to mock the idea that something can be "true for me" (since, I thought, the very concept of "truth" demands that if something is true, it is true for everyone at all times), I recognize now that that smugness was the result of treating all claims like scientific claims and making no room for the softer, more liquid, narrative-based kinds of claims like "Once upon a time," "A long time ago in a galaxy far, far away," or "In the beginning was the Word." Knowledge is a tricky thing—I can *know* that two plus two equals four, but I am only ever *getting to know* others and myself.

What's true of us as individuals is also true of us collectively. When a primitive tribesman relays his people's origin myth, it is not intended to be understood according to the rigid rules of science or historiography. Whether we're talking about the Bantu, the Cherokee, the Hebrew, or the modern Christian, the narrative they tell that contextualizes and legitimatizes them stands above the kind of crass scrutiny that certain scientific and historical claims demand. The original tellers of these tales didn't intend for their narratives to be fact-checked according to our modern standards of "truth-hood." They just sort of heard them and passed them on and understood themselves in their light. Now, of course, the strict atheist will dismiss all this with a wave of his hand, because at the end of the day, he, like the religious zealots he spends his life debating on the Internet, is a fundamentalist. He inhabits a black-and-white world of scientific facts with no loose ends, a closed system with no ambiguity. There is no supernatural, only natural; there is no metaphysical, only physical; there is no messiness, only tidiness. All questions about the world either have been or will be answered by science, and any claims about God, the soul, or the afterlife are eye-rolled at and cast aside as the results of superstition and priestcraft.

Here's the thing, though: Stuff like "the meaning of life" is kind of above the scientist's pay grade. Science's job is to teach us about the physical world: How long has the earth been here? Where did man come from? What's the deal with this rash on my thigh? And we would do well to listen when science speaks on such matters (especially the rash thing, you really need to get that looked at). But to assume that because science can answer some questions, it therefore can answer all of them is silly. (And to dismiss as irrelevant all questions that demand nonscientific answers is even worse.) As human beings, we have a natural curiosity to learn about ourselves and the world around us—and not just the scientific stuff about how our hearts pump blood through our veins (as fascinating as that may be) but also about how our hearts fill with joy at the oddest of times (like when a memory is triggered by a scent or a song, or when Jaynie bats her eyelashes at me). And that curiosity about the deeper and more mysterious aspects of existence is what stories are for. That's when the hushed tones and wonder come out, that's when we feel the need to see ourselves as characters in a larger cosmic drama, and that's when anything less hopeful and sublime than "and they lived happily ever after" simply won't do.

And in my case (and it may be different in yours), it was Catholicism that made mystery and magic and medievalism safe. It really hit me a couple of years ago. I had recently begun dabbling in Catholic stuff and allowing myself to be challenged by all things Roman, when I came across an article by a former seminary professor called "Harry Potter and the Allure of a Magical World." It argued that medieval Europe, like Harry Potter's England, was fraught with too much otherworldliness and mysticism, and that one of the triumphs of the Reformation in the sixteenth century was ridding the ecclesial landscape of all that blasted magical and metaphysical mumbo jumbo. Sacraments that actually worked, priests who could do stuff to natural things to make them supernatural, and humanity becoming divine were all just carryovers from a superstitious and simplistic time before there was even a printing press, and it was the newly emerged Protestantism that broke the spell. Thus Europe was "disenchanted," Narnia was cast out of Naples, and Heidelberg was finally rid of Hogwarts. Thanks to the Enlightenment and its Protestant offspring, *hoc est corpus* was dismissed as *hocus-pocus*.

But really? *Really?* Is this really what we want—the genie safely back in the bottle, the wardrobe bolted shut, and the spellbinding expelled? Can we really be content with a clinical, anesthetized world that safely quarantines anything disruptive or sublime out of sight and out of mind? Please, can we not? Because for my part, an existence that is devoid of meaning, souls, or anything beyond our mindless animalistic selves doesn't just deny every intrinsic and intuitive thing we feel about the world, it also sounds really boring. We are more than mere biological machines—we are human persons, and we need to feel connected in a real, existential way with that part of us that transcends the mere earthy and earthly. And to my mind, it is narrative that helps us do that. We're not meant to be atomized, ghettoized, or isolated, and seeing ourselves as coparticipants in a grander saga, as fellows in common folklore, far from being a forced imposition on how we naturally think, actually gives expression to what we already know deep down.

Ritual, Beatitude, and Anarchist Theology

The issue of *narrative* leads quite naturally to the matter of *ritual*. All communities, whether religious or not, have certain rituals they enact. (Often those rituals are so ingrained in the fiber of those communities that the participants rarely notice just how bizarre they really are.) For example, each year millions of Americans gather together in large settings to watch grown men in tight pants chew tobacco and play a game involving wooden sticks and words like "Two away in the bottom of the fourth, runners on the corners, the count oh and two to the clean-up hitter who's one for one on the day with a couple of RBIs." And then for some reason, at precisely the 6½/9 mark of the game, everyone stands up and sings a song about peanuts. I know, right? WTF? But that's just it: Baseball is a kind of folk culture with its own rules, garb, and distinct lexicon (which is why even a native English speaker from a non-American country won't have any idea what that quote above means, despite understanding all the words).

Or consider weddings. Two people love each other and desire to spend their lives together, so what do they do? Well, naturally, they (1) gather together on a Saturday in a church or a ballroom of some kind, (2) put on uncomfortable ridiculous-looking clothes that they will never wear again, (3) walk down an aisle at an awkwardly slow pace, (4) repeat some words that some guy tells them to say because he got a piece of paper from the Internet that authorizes him to lead the ceremony, (5) give each other a piece of jewelry (which is sometimes carried into the hall on a pillow by a toddler), (6) and then kiss, both at the end of the ceremony itself and at the meal afterward, whenever someone arbitrarily decides to tap his fork against his champagne glass. Why do these lovers do this? It's so obvious! Because that's what people in love do. *Duh.*

It's no different with religion. Since the dawn of time, worshippers have gathered together in sacred assemblies to invoke the gods, to burn their treasured possessions in priestly offerings, and to hear their prophets divulge the arcane mysteries of the divine: that patience is a virtue, that all you need is love, that you reap what you sow, and that we're one but we're not the same. And like the baseball fan and wedding attender, the worshipper enacts certain rituals that express the unique narrative of his own tribe. Now, when we are exposed to the strange rituals of foreign religionists, we often scoff or roll our eyes at how odd they look. "Why does she wear that scarf on her head?" "Why do they face that direction to pray?" "Why do they celebrate those weird holy days?" Of course, as with baseball and weddings, we rarely appreciate the oddity of our own rituals and behave as if hiding colored eggs that come from a magical bunny on an ever-changing Sunday each spring because a Galilean carpenter supposedly came back to life after his execution two thousand years ago makes all the sense in the world.

Catholic Christianity has rituals aplenty. It has bishops in pointy hats (who we believe are successors of the original twelve apostles) who can turn bread and wine into the body and blood of Christ, which we then eat and drink. It has periods during which we are supposed to fast and give up doing perfectly legitimate and fun things. And it has a whole lot of kneeling and hand motions that everyone seems to know when to perform without being told. Like calling in a southpaw from the bullpen or throwing uncooked rice at a couple because we're supposedly happy for them, these religious rituals are weird. But the thing is, doing weird things is kind of constitutive of our humanity, and enacting liturgies (whether sacred or secular) is part and parcel of who we are. As grasping and childish and short-of-the-mark as we surely are when engaging in spiritual acts, we engage in them still (and we must), because deep within us—perhaps buried—is the nagging notion that beatitude is the destiny of the species.

Now, if we are meant for beatitude and ultimate happiness (which most of us instinctively think is true), then it becomes incumbent on us to find a *creed,* a *code,* and a *cult* that grounds this idea and gives real, concrete expression to it. If life, when all is said and done, has actual meaning and purpose, then doesn't it make sense that we would seek out some combination of beliefs (creed), morals (code), and spiritual rituals (cult) that will help us live out this hope in a way that is embodied and practical?

Now, I know what some of you may be thinking, because it is precisely what I would have thought not too long ago: "You're supposed to develop your ideas and practices from your theology, not the other way around." In other words, shouldn't we start with God and then move forward from there? Is it really okay to begin with some human instinct (in this case, that we will live happily ever after) and then reverse-engineer a theology to justify it? Aren't we doing things from the bottom up rather than the top down? Isn't this approach way more human than divine? I suppose so, but I have a couple of excuses for this seeming breach of etiquette and protocol. First, culturally speaking my default mode is pretty much one of anarchy. By that I don't mean chaos or mayhem but simply that society works best when it is organized from the ground up rather than things being forced upon us from on high. So doing theology in this way makes sense to me: We start with earth, with what we intuitively know "on the ground" and "in the trenches," and work our way up to the higher and more heavenly stuff. (Remember: Grace perfects nature, but nature also sets the stage for grace.)

But second and more important, the faults and failings in my own life have sort of demanded this kind of approach. There was a time when I really did feel like I had it all figured out, and it seemed like Christianity could have a fairy tale ending for me even if it would be a nightmare for others. My ideas about God were all biblical and therefore correct, and my personal life reflected how awesome I was (outwardly anyway), so what did I care if existence for other people was a devilish tragedy rather than a divine comedy? What skin was taken off my back by the idea that no beatitude or blessing awaited the bulk of the morally or theologically incorrect masses? *I* was one of the elect, *I* had lived a life free of scandal, *I* had a solid track record of standing up for the Truth. So despite the fact that I was dying inside, a hollow ghost in whom the last traces of humanity had all but rotted away, at least I was orthodox. But when my personal and professional life went to shite, the unbending and inflexible God of pure will started to seem more like Zeus or Judge Judy than a compassionate Father. So there I was, standing amid the ruins of my former life, and the collapse was all my own doing. At that point I felt completely lost, and God seemed a stranger at best, a fiction at worst. Everything I thought I knew was now up in the air, while I myself felt pinned to the ground with a mountain of guilt and confusion sitting on my chest.

At that point, if I was going to continue trying to believe, I needed to rebuild. So beginning with the faith statement that "life has meaning," I began to retrofit a series of other ideas that justified my hope. If things like the birth of a child and romantic love are as powerful and sublime as most of us consider them to be (and the loss of them as tragic), there must be some reason for this. And you guessed it—this is where the "fairy tale" part comes in.

As adults we dismiss fairy tales as childish and juvenile, but to echo G. K. Chesterton (as you have noticed, one of my favorite writers), it is grown-ups and not kids who need fairy tales, since kids are content with just tales.[1] You don't have to tell a child there's a magical treasure inside that box—you can just tell them there's a box. (Seriously, parents, just give your kid a cardboard box, and he will entertain himself for hours. There, I just saved you hundreds of dollars at Christmas. When that stops working, just throw him some Tupperware or something, and he'll be happy as a clam, and you can go back to whatever you were doing.) But the older

---

1. I will be echoing Chesterton, using my own words, for a little while here. I don't think he'd mind.

we get, the more "sophisticated" we become. This means that we slowly lose that basic sense of childhood wonder and awe at the ordinary things of life, and we become bored. We no longer fawn—we yawn. So we need tales about golden apples because we've lost that sense of astonishment at their being red, and we tell myths about rivers running with wine because it no longer moves us that they run with water.

But I didn't want to become a cynic. I didn't want my life to devolve into a detached, dispassionate ceasefire with the world. Or worse, I didn't want to become some smug atheist who slow-blinks at people when they mention transcendent beauty or souls or the meaning of life. I wanted to retain an element of childlikeness (which is how Jesus said we are supposed to be in order to see the heavenly kingdom). I wanted wonder and needed naïveté. I simply had to believe that behind our narratives there was a Narrator, and that the fundamental, gut-level, gun-to-our-head instinct that there is something more out there is true: "There are fairy godmothers because there are godmothers. And there are godmothers because there is God."

God the Archetypal Storyteller

As I focused on this idea that humans are narrative beings who root ourselves in stories (whether cosmic, local, or both), it dawned on me that if there is a divine Storyteller, then every tale must be derivative of that one big story he is telling. And moreover (here's where it became personal for me), if *God* is telling that one big story, it must be pretty damn good. Unlike, say, *Purple Rain*. Have you ever seen *Purple Rain*? Probably not. Neither had I, but then Prince died, and I was feeling all nostalgic, so I watched it a month or so ago. It was hands down one of the worst and most pointless films ever made. The actual story would have taken about four minutes to tell, but once they added all the drawn-out driving sequences, overacting, and musical performances by Morris Day and the Time, they were able to stretch the thing out into a full-length film and gross $68 million at the box office. (The soundtrack is incredible, though.)

Now, if God is the ultimate storyteller behind all our personal and cultural tales, then that story must be the archetype and standard by which all human stories are evaluated. And it seems to me that we all really do have an innate sense of what makes a good story and what makes a bad one. This is why most tales have some version of a happy ending where the girl gets the boy, the cops catch the robbers, and the guys in the white hats prevail. This being the case, then, a couple of issues arose in my mind. For example, would that primal and standard-setting "greatest story ever told" include something like eternal conscious torment in hell?

I mean, did God call together all his most trusted angelic advisers up in heaven and say, "Okay, I'm experiencing writer's block here. I have this idea where I just mercilessly torture people for trillions of years—maybe skinning them alive slowly or something—after which time I am no closer to being done than when I started (and not because I *have* to, I'm sort of *forced* to do it because they refused to believe in me, which for some reason I never gave them a chance to do). Should I put that in? Yes? Okay, gotcha. But should I maybe lessen the time frame on the relentless torment thing? Like maybe have it only last a few thousand years? You know what, forget I asked, I like the 'for all eternity' part and I'm keeping it in. Meeting adjourned!"

I realize I'm being somewhat cavalier, but it seems to me that if God exists, is telling our story, and is both good and in control of its outcome, then he would choose to have the story *not* include the skinning-people-alive-slowly-for-all-eternity part. Call me a hopeless romantic, but that's just how I see it.

Consider another example. If God is good and a good storyteller, would he opt for orchestrating a situation in which it is really *likely* that people come to know him, or really *rare*? Because when we look at the world as it is, the majority of humankind lives in areas where the Christian message is not known. And to make matters worse, this is the case not just with the world as it is but with the world as it has always been. If you were born in Yemen in 2005, or in the Americas in 1200, or anywhere outside the Middle East in Anytime B.C., you're pretty much screwed if the story God is telling includes the unfortunate provision that in order to be a recipient of divine grace, you need to join Team Jesus. And continuing to push the issue, if you were a "savage" in the days before the printing press and widespread literacy, the chances you'd get to hear a bit of orthodox theology were slim to nonexistent. After all, there were no affordable Bibles, you couldn't read them if there were, and even if a group of Europeans did brave the transoceanic voyage to try to save you, they'd most likely either die in the attempt or end up enslaving or killing you when they arrived. I don't know about you, but this story sucks.

While some conservative believers make room in their thinking for the whole "God will accept people based on their response to the light they've been given" idea, many do not. For the more hardcore ones, God is perfectly just in consigning to eternal perdition all who failed to accept Jesus even if they never had the chance to do so, because Adam ate the apple. (Remember that part from before? Where we are all on the hook for his disobedience and are utterly abhorrent to God from the moment we are conceived?) So according to this schema, millions and millions of people will be hurled headlong into hell because they didn't believe in a God whom through no fault of their own they never knew existed. And moreover, this God in whom they didn't believe could easily have made himself known to them, but he chose not to and then punished them for it. Call me crazy, but this is just the worst story ever. Like, if this were a major motion picture and the "God" character were a human, he'd be the villain whom we'd all be waiting for the hero to vanquish.

Now, I can hear my former self responding to this, and I know precisely what he would say: "Sorry, but you don't get to judge God according to your own human standards or hold the Almighty accountable to what you think is fair. After all, his ways are higher than our ways, and we just have to trust him." The problem with this approach is that it leaves out the central trait that characterizes God and manifests who he ultimately is: love. As Paul said, "So now faith, hope, and love abide, these three; but the greatest of these is love" (1 Cor. 13:13), and as John insisted, "Anyone who does not love does not know God, because God is love. . . . So we have come to know and to believe the love that God has for us. God is love, and whoever abides in love abides in God, and God abides in him" (1 John 4:8, 16). Love is who God is, it is where he is to be found, it is what constitutes him and makes him present. Where love is, God is; and where love isn't, God has left the building.

This means that any claim that God's ways are "higher" than ours necessarily entails the idea that his ways are *more loving* than ours. If the "greatest of [all virtues] is love," then to whatever degree God is greater than we, to that degree he is more loving than we. Therefore it is an utter betrayal of God's loving nature to insist that, while we humans would never be so seemingly unloving as to withhold ourselves from our children and then punish them for it, God will do exactly this because, after all, his ways are higher than ours. According to this way of thinking, "higher" is tantamount to "more sadistic and villainous." Another way to put it is to say that the loftiness of God is not intended to make him more of an asshole.

This notion that the "higher" nature of God's ways explains why he would do seemingly cruel things to his children that we earthly fathers would never do to ours also flies in the face of the idea, so central to my own misfit faith and to the Catholic tradition more broadly, that grace perfects nature. As I have argued already, the relationship of grace to nature, divinity to humanity, and heaven to earth is not one of antagonism or threat but one of redemption and fulfillment. We know this is true because, according to theologians way smarter than I will ever be, the divinity of Christ did not swallow or eclipse his humanity—it perfected it. Thus the risen and ascended Christ is not some co-opted demi-human cobbled together from the scraps of the failed first model, like Anakin Skywalker after he became Darth Vader: "More machine now than man." No, the risen Christ did not become "more divine now than man," as though those two natures were at odds with each other. In fact, the risen Christ is the prototype for what true humanity is—he is more human than we are precisely because of, and not in spite of, his divinity. To quote the apostle John once more: "Beloved, we are God's children now, and what we will be has not yet appeared; but we know that when he appears we shall be like him, because we shall see him as he is" (1 John 3:2).

Here's the radical takeaway: If God is the ultimate storyteller, and if our instincts about what makes a story good are to be trusted since grace perfects nature, then it is perfectly legitimate to hopefully affirm something about the divine story simply on the basis that it makes the story better. Now, there are caveats and qualifications coming, so relax. But for now just consider what I am proposing: When all is said and done and the dust from the divine love affair with earth has settled, if the story was improved by there being no part about everlasting retributive vengeance, or if the absence of the idea that salvation will be enjoyed by only a precious and select few makes the narrative less nefarious, then for those reasons alone, we can affirm such things in hope. The very nature of God as a loving Father is all the rationale we need for believing that the gospel is a tale more broadly redeeming and lovingly unifying than can be imagined by the minds of even earth's most tenderhearted storytellers. Yeah, yeah, I know: All this hippie "Kumbaya" stuff is so, well, *weak*. But so what? The bloodthirsty cage-fighter Jesus of American fundamentalism has done enough damage. Plus, he's almost as much of a prick as those who invented him. (And last I checked, weakness is kind of God's whole thing.)

Suffering, Strings Attached, and Conditional Joy

This idea—that grace perfecting nature and God's loving fatherhood are sufficient grounds to believe that the gospel is at least as good a story as we can imagine—invites an important question: What are we to make of life's struggles? After all, I can "imagine" a life in which there are no hardships or temptations, and in which nothing expected of me is in the least bit uncomfortable. That sounds pretty good now that I think about it. If God is supposed to be telling not only a good story but the best one possible, why isn't he telling the one where everything is super chill and I can just kind of coast along without a speed bump or a care in the world?

Here again fairy tales can help. All good fairy tales include at least two elements: a peculiar set of circumstances, and a peculiar set of conditions for enjoying them. For example, Cinderella wants to join her stepsisters at the royal ball, but she can't because she has nothing to wear (hashtag WhitePeopleProblems). So what happens? A fairy godmother magically appears and solves her issue, clothing her in an exquisite gown and furnishing her with a coach and driver. But then the condition: She must leave the party no later than midnight, or else her dress will turn back into rags and her coach will turn back into a pumpkin. Or consider a (slightly) more contemporary example: *Pretty Woman,* the 1990 film starring Julia Roberts and Richard Gere.[2] A wealthy businessman hires a beautiful prostitute to be his escort and companion. He showers her with gifts and clothing, takes her to fancy events, and makes her feel like a princess. But once his week of business in Los Angeles is concluded, her

2. To be honest, I barely remembered the details of this movie, but thankfully many of my female friends on Facebook have an encyclopedic knowledge of it. Thanks Claire, Nicole, Jenipher, Sarah, Heather, Serena, and Karye Ann!

services are no longer needed, and she has to vacate his penthouse and go back to her normal life. In both "Cinderella" and *Pretty Woman,* a strange set of circumstances arises, with conditions attached that may seem rather random (certainly in the case of Cinderella, and in *Pretty Woman* the conditions become more arbitrary as the film progresses and the two main characters fall in love).

Now, can you imagine Cinderella objecting to the conditions under which her fairy godmother has placed her? "Wait—what? I have to leave the dance by *midnight*? That's kind of lame." To this complaint, her fairy godmother would probably respond, "Oh I'm sorry, is my magical spell too inconvenient for you? Would you rather not go at all and just be the filthy slave girl you were when I showed up? Because how's that working out for you?" And then she would mutter something under her breath about how kids these days are such entitled little shits. No, the wonder of the arrangement makes the conditions deal-with-able. Cinderella would never have balked at the restrictions placed upon her, because they were imposed by the same magic that created the context for them in the first place. The two things were linked, so to whine about one of them would be both ironic and ungrateful.

A similar magic is at play in our own lives as participants in the story God is telling. If we can de-sophisticate ourselves enough to recognize the sheer wonder of the everyday and ordinary, then the occasional restriction or expectation attached to those enjoyments will hardly seem harsh.

Chesterton called this "the doctrine of conditional joy," and by that he meant that fairy tales merely reflect the way the world actually works. So it's not that God arbitrarily withholds his blessings until we jump through some random hoop he has set up for us (like a parent withholding dessert from a child until he finishes his vegetables, or a man not letting his dog eat the treat he placed on the ground until he gives it the verbal go-ahead). Rather, attaching certain conditions or expectations to some good thing, or drawing boundaries around it, provides the context in which that blessing can be enjoyed. It's not accidental or arbitrary, it's real and built in (meaning that's just how the world sort of is). The command to love your neighbor by sharing with him from the bounty of your own wealth is not some external condition attached to having wealth—it is the way wealth can be enjoyably had. The condition creates the capacity to enjoy the blessing, and removing the condition just mucks everything up.

Take sex, for example. (There, got your attention back, didn't I?) Many people see sex as nothing more than the mere scratching of a biological itch and consider any restrictions on it to be but forced and ad hoc societal conventions, holdovers from a more puritanical past. Yet I can't help but wonder whether such a person, far from truly loving and enjoying sex, has actually become numb to the wonder of it. Going back to my earlier point about being in awe of ordinary things, if sex were considered to be as magical a thing as attending the ball was for Cinderella, then the suggestion that it be enjoyed in the context of a committed and loving relationship would quite likely seem perfectly reasonable. Thus the feeling would not be "I have to have sex with someone I *love*?" but "I *get* to love someone and have *sex* with them too?" In other words, when we discover that the same magic that makes sex possible also creates the boundaries in which it is intended to happen, the boundary will seem less like an electric barbed-wire fence and more like the wall around a playground.

This is what monks and mystics call *asceticism,* a term that derives from the Latin word for "discipline" or "practice" (and was originally applied to athletes in training). The point of rules and restrictions was never to create some artificial and capricious circumstance that merely adds unnecessary hindrances to pleasure. On the contrary, *it was to train us for joy.* When it comes to having wealth, having sex, or having bourbon, the goal is not to rid ourselves of regulations but to discover the wonder and magic of such things, to the point where we prize them enough never to squander them or consider them common. And the way to ascribe value to a thing is to not overindulge in it—which is why you don't chug mouthfuls of twenty-three-year-old Pappy Van Winkle straight from the bottle unless you're some classless and uncouth philistine. No, you sniff it first, then sip it and roll it around on your tongue, tasting the nutty, caramel notes, and then you swallow. It doesn't take a genius with a doctorate in human psychology to know that the person who slams shot after shot of whiskey, or who bangs a different college coed every night, or who hoards material possessions has long since stopped experiencing any true enjoyment from these things. They have lost their charm and become disgraceful (dis-graceful, get it?). Thus pursuits that were once viewed with wonder are now, because of the sad spiral from *use* to *overuse,* mere coping mechanisms and occasions for *abuse.* As Chesterton said, "We should thank God for beer and Burgundy by not drinking too much of them." Elsewhere he chastised the notorious libertine Oscar Wilde for insisting that sunsets have no value since we cannot pay for them. *Pish posh,* Chesterton retorted: "We can pay for sunsets! We can pay for them by not being Oscar Wilde."

The key to all this, of course, is love. Love is what transforms restraint from something unnecessary, heartless, and austere into something devotional, sacrificial, and adoring. Imagine if in some future time romance goes out of style, to the point where none of the things we now associate with it are ever done. If they consult their history books and read about us today, they will say something like, "Geez, what was wrong with those coldhearted twenty-first-century women? I mean, demanding men give them flowers? Exacting tribute in the form of jewelry? What cruel and rigid tyrants those females were!" And without the central component of love, this would be a pretty reasonable assessment. But if they understood that men undertook such actions not out of a sense of constraint or fear but out of love, it would change the entire picture. Likewise with God. He desires mercy over sacrifice, devotion over duty, and love over mere law keeping.

But here's the good news: While true love always involves suffering, true love also redeems that suffering. When a man gives an engagement ring to his future bride, the cost associated with it no longer stings his pocketbook when she accepts his proposal. Likewise, when God's story involves our suffering, divine love transforms that hardship into opportunities to express our devotion and to be trained for joy. Like Cinderella leaving the ball a bit earlier than she probably wanted to, when for Jesus's sake I say no to excessive, conspicuous consumption or endure some criticism for refusing to repay evil for evil because it makes me look weak, I will bear these marks with deep joy. Just as the wounds in the flesh of the risen Christ are no longer ugly but beautiful, so it is with us and the scars we bear. Whether we are exercising restraint or enduring great cost, it only causes resentment if love is forgotten and the one for whom these tasks are undertaken is obscured. But when we remember that the divine story is also a love story, then the sacrifice and suffering we endure are not only infinitely worthwhile but also tokens themselves of divine love.

I Want It All

The life of faith, then, is a life of feasting and fasting, indulgence and restraint (and in my case, much more of the former and nowhere near enough of the latter). As Ecclesiastes's Preacher proclaimed, "For everything there is a season . . . a time to weep, and a time to laugh; a time to mourn, and a time to dance" (3:1, 4). Speaking personally, I spent much of my life trying to navigate a maze of either/ors, pursuing pretty relentlessly a life and theology with few loose ends and minimal messiness. And adding to that burden was the need to do so publicly, as a Minister of the Word and Sacraments in the Presbyterian Church. If I contradicted myself in my writings, someone would find it. If I made a slightly offensive (but hilarious) comment on a blog, someone would give me a talking-to. If my life smacked more of humanity than of divinity, I would feel the suspicion. And as I have mentioned already, I had been in some form of Christian leadership or another since I was in high school, and at a certain point it just became too much.

The door into Catholicism, it turned out, was also a gateway into a misfit faith and new way of doing spirituality that feels very different from what came before. Because the central issue for everything is Christ and the Incarnation, it's kind of hard to insist on an either/or type of worldview. Is Christ divine or is he human? *Yes* (which is why I am much more comfortable these days with both/ands than I am with either/ors). This liberty has freed me from the need to place everything into neat, well-defined categories that never conflict or contradict. So when someone asks me how I can affirm *this* while also saying *that*, I can just shrug and say, "I have no idea, and the ambiguity of what I am saying will cost me absolutely no sleep tonight."

Is misfit faith about love or suffering? Feasting or fasting? Divinity or humanity? Heaven or earth? The answer is yes, to all of it. And yeah, I want it all: the now and the later, the spirit and the flesh, the head, the heart, and the stations of the cross. I would rather embrace way too much than way too little, because something tells me that as wide as I can open my and arms and heart, God's are always open wider.

Acknowledgments

I'm not going to lie; this book was not a pleasure to write. It was incredibly painful, actually, and I am convinced that without all the encouragement and support I received along the way it never would have seen the light of day.

Many thanks to the whole team at Penguin Random House, and to Gary Jansen in particular. His willingness to adjust expectations (and deadlines) to fit my spiritual schizophrenia has been indispensable to this project.

Thank you as well to Ainsley, Maddoc, and Fiona for the opportunity to be the best dad I know how to be.

To Fr. Kurt Nagel, whose spiritual guidance during a time of personal upheaval will never be forgotten.

Much gratitude to Scott Hahn and Mark Shea for their patience and mentorship during the transition out of my former ministry.

And finally, heartfelt thanks and love to Jaynie, whose unwavering encouragement has kept me going when everything in me told me to quit. You're the strongest person I know.

ABOUT THE AUTHOR

JASON J. STELLMAN, cohost of the podcast *Drunk Ex-Pastors*, is a Southern California native and transplant to Seattle, who wishes he still lived in Europe. He served as a missionary with Calvary Chapel of Costa Mesa in Uganda (1991–92) and in Hungary (1994–2000). Ordained in the Presbyterian Church in America, he was called to plant Exile Presbyterian Church in the Seattle area where he served from 2004 to 12. In September 2012, he was received into the Catholic Church. He drinks and questions his faith regularly.